Modern Military Powers
ISRAEL

The Military Press
First English edition published by Temple Press
an imprint of Newnes Books 1984

This 1984 edition published by The Military Press
and distributed by Crown Publishers, Inc.
hgfedcba

Printed and bound in Italy

Created and produced by Stan Morse
Aerospace Publishing Ltd
10 Barley Mow Passage
London W4 4PH
England
© Copyright Aerospace Publishing Ltd 1984

Aircraft colour profiles © Pilot Press Ltd

All correspondence concerning the content of this volume
should be addressed to Aerospace Publishing Ltd. Trade
enquiries should be addressed to The Military Press, One
Park Avenue, New York, NY 10016.

ISBN: 0-517-41483X

Library of Congress Catalog Card Number: 83-62996

Artists: Keith Fretwell
 Tony Gibbons
 The Art Workshop
 Ray Hutchins
Authors: Terry Gander, Bernard Ireland,
 Paul A. Jackson

Typesetting: SX Composing Ltd, Rayleigh, Essex
Colour origination: Imago Publishing Ltd, Thame, Oxon

Contents

Modern Military Powers

ISRAEL

General Editor: Stan Morse

The Military Press
New York

The Tormented Birth of Israel

During its short history, the modern state of Israel has fought no less than four major wars and numerous minor conflicts, from counter-guerrilla to full-scale military operations; to date Israel has emerged victorious through all of them. Always outnumbered in men and equipment, the Israelis have demonstrated time and again their remarkable fighting abilities that have placed them in the Valhalla of warriors. But their beginnings were very modest, and their strength is still numerically weak, yet they have survived.

Left: *Ha-Shomer* members in 1913. Originally a society of watchmen, *ha-Shomer* was transformed into an armed self-defence body as a result of attacks on Jewish settlements in Ottoman-ruled Palestine.

Below: The Balfour declaration and rising Jewish immigration generated tension between Jew and Arab which turned into violence. The *Haganah* (Defence) was formed in the 1930s as a clandestine Jewish militia.

The biblical state of Israel was no stranger to armed conflict, as even a short perusal of the Old Testament will reveal, but when the Romans inflicted the Diaspora (dispersion) on the Palestinian Jews during the 1st century AD the Jews ceased to be a nation and became a race scattered to the four corners of the known world. As they scattered the Jews took with them their religion, and despite the dispersion this religion proved to be as tenacious as it had ever been. And with the religion lasted the yearning to return to a new Israel situated in the land of Palestine.

The dream persisted through the centuries, but it was not until the 1880s that the first determined attempts to return in force on an organized basis were attempted. These early attempts foundered amid a welter of poor living conditions and the resultant disease, but more efforts were made and by 1910 the first effective wave of Jewish immigration to Palestine was well established. These earlier immigrants had a very hard life as they were forced to settle in areas that were shunned by the Arab populace. At that time this land was mainly in the marshy plains of Palestine, for

The Tormented Birth of Israel

Pinat Ha-Shomer, 1938, and a training course for *Haganah* instructors is under way. Prior to World War II, *Haganah* members received basic infantry training, together with instruction in relatively simple tactical manoeuvres.

the Arabs maintained their main centres of population in the hills. From their hard work they prospered and their numbers grew until by the period following World War I they were established in appreciable numbers.

Unfortunately for the settlers, that period was marked by political change and upheaval. Despite the promises of the Balfour Declaration, the post-war treaties dealing with the wreckage of the old Turkish Empire handed over much of the territory desired by the Zionist settlers to the emergent Arab nations. As if this were not enough the new Arab rulers thought they had reason to suspect the Jewish immigrants of plotting to occupy Jerusalem and other religious centres by force, so by the late 1920s attacks on Jews and on Jewish property and land were becoming commonplace.

Despite the growing troubles more and more Jewish immigrants made their way to Palestine, determined to put down roots and stay. More and more land was taken over by purchase or settlement in barren areas until the resident Arabs began to feel themselves caught in a process of dispossession. Attacks grew in number and severity to the point where the Jews

started to form themselves into organized self-defence forces.

The very first Jewish self-defence force was the *ha-Shomer* (watchman), which was formed as early as 1909. These were the 'Watchmen' that were to pass into Israeli history, but their defence function was also infused with a strong socialist tendency that had small appeal to many settlers, and by 1920 the *ha-Shomer* was no more.

But the passing of the body left a void that had to be filled as the need for some form of self-defence grew year by year. The local police forces were often pro-Arab, and the few military forces in the area were few and widely scattered. Thus the Jews had to fend for themselves and organized themselves into a body known as the *Haganah*, a body that can lay claim to having been the founder of the modern IDF/A. At first, and for years afterwards, arms for the new force were difficult to obtain and so few in number. Things were made no easier by the reluctance of the British administration to accept the concept of an armed body that was outside their control, and the *Haganah* soon went under-

Vans and trucks were used by *Haganah* mobile guard units for patrol duties, and where necessary were converted into simple armoured cars by adding steel plates to the body.

Far right: March 1947, and Jerusalem has been under 24-hour curfew. A machete-armed British soldier moves past an assembly area after a brief relaxation of the curfew to enable citizens to obtain food.

ground. For some years it remained a loose association of local groups with little central control. The *Haganah's* activities were purely defensive and consisted mainly of patrolling its own farms and localities, lack of weapons preventing anything more ambitious. Gradually the loose associations grew in number and were slowly centralized under the guidance of a body of leaders and suppliers, but despite this in 1929 large-scale anti-Jewish riots broke out, to the extent that some areas had to be vacated by their Jewish settlers. These areas remained under Arab control until after 1967.

The *Haganah* had thus failed its first real test and in the years immediately after 1929 its internal structure underwent some drastic upheavals, to the point where for some years it was fragmented and disorganized. But events overtook these internal troubles as more and more Jewish settlers arrived, partly as the result of the nascent policies of Hitler and the Nazi party in central Europe. The new arrivals established new settlements along important routes, swelled the numbers of the *Haganah*, and brought with them military and other skills that would stand them in good stead in the future. The British at one point accepted the increasing numbers by allowing the settlers to form their own police force under British control. This was the Supernumerary Police Force which was soon transformed into a front for the *Haganah*, who used the rifles and training provided for its own ends. The police grew into the Jewish Settlement Police (JSP), a mobile force using trucks and even some armoured vehicles, and this too came under *Haganah* influence.

By the late 1930s the political divides that bedevil Israeli society to this day were making themselves apparent. The role of the *Haganah* was essentially defensive, but factions among the settlers wanted to impose a more drastic counter to the various attacks on Jewish life and property that were becoming more frequent. Various underground gangs started to inflict their own revenge on the Arabs. Some of these underground gangs had their activities organized by political factions, but they faded from the scene by 1940, their

place being taken by a new force inspired by a British soldier, Captain Orde Wingate.

Although a Christian, Wingate was also a Zionist and put his considerable abilities at the service of the *Haganah*. In many ways the present boldness and mobility of the modern IDF/A can be traced back to the philosophy of Wingate, for although his ideas proved to be a disaster in conventional war (as the later Chindit campaigns in Burma were to prove) they were ideal for the *Haganah*. Under his guidance new groups known as Special Night Squads, or SNS, sprang up to take the fight to the enemy, to establish secure communications

The 700-ton steamer *San Dimitrio* with 1,279 illegal immigrants aboard. Intercepted at sea by the Royal Navy, she had to be assisted into Haifa before being boarded for fear of capsizing the dangerously overloaded vessel. The passengers were transferred to internment camps on Cyprus.

The Tormented Birth of Israel

In the independence struggle, the *Haganah* had not only to contend with hostile Arab forces and the ruling British, but with dissident Jewish groups, described with some justification as terrorists by the British administration. These groups, such as the Stern 'gang' and Irgun Zvai Leumi, were not subject to *Haganah* or to the Jewish Agency, and were responsible for such outrages as the bombing of the King David Hotel in Tel Aviv. The photograph shows a second bomb exploding at the hotel.

and to remove Arab terrorists from Jewish-settled areas. Many of the leaders of the later IDF/A had their early experiences and training in the SNS, and their approach to conflict was affected in no small way by Wingate and his teachings.

With the coming of World War II events in Palestine started to move more rapidly. At first the British forces in Palestine and the Jewish settlers were in close accord and some settlers even joined the Allies in uniform. By the early 1940s the once-scattered settlers had joined together into a loose form of self-government, and with this evolution the *Haganah* grew in influence and size, although not in weapon strength. Finally it grew in strength to the point at which the

British felt compelled to institute a campaign against the *Haganah*, starting a series of arms searches and imprisonments that turned the bulk of the settlers against them. By 1944 the Stern Group was established to attack the British forces, and from then until 1949 they remained a thorn in the side of the 'occupying forces', as the British came increasingly to be known.

Various other small units joined the Stern Group and by 1945 even the *Haganah* was openly working against the British. By late 1945 an organized programme of attacks against communications and other such targets was under way. This programme was undertaken as the result of the realization that the British were unwilling to undertake their part in the establishment of a

Survivors are helped from the wreckage of the King David Hotel. Casualties were heavy, as the building which served as British headquarters was wrecked by terrorist bombs.

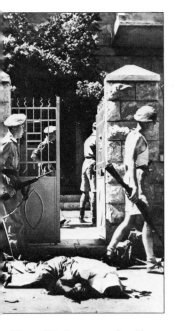

Above: Attacks were made with increasing frequency upon the British. Here, troops pass the body of an unsuccessful attacker, shot dead while attacking barracks in Jerusalem.

Above right: As preparations for the birth of the state of Israel went ahead, *Haganah* members practised with whatever weapons they could muster, in this case a long-obsolete Lewis gun which has been stripped of its barrel cooling jacket.

formal Jewish state and that any such state could only come about as the result of the Jews' own efforts.

After 1945 mass immigration began on a scale hitherto unknown, and with the masses of refugees from the upheavals of post-war Europe came money, experience and men to swell the numbers of the *Haganah*. With the growth in numbers there came the growth in importance of a force known as the *Palmach*, a force that would grow in importance out of all proportion to its numbers. The *Palmach* became the elite of the *Haganah*, being a body formed of small units that moved and fought with skill, lethality and swiftness. They worked on the settlements by day and fought their enemies by night and from their ranks grew yet

another element in the modern IDF/A, an element of self-reliance, self-confidence and military skills allied with a fierce political motivation that would impose its mark on the future state. Many later leaders of Israeli life served in the *Palmach*.

By late 1947 the United Nations took a hand in Palestine and announced that the Jews were to be given the opportunity to form their own nation. The surrounding Arab nations, not surprisingly, opposed any such thing and in their turn announced that they would fight any imposed political institution. For all that, the preparations for the new state of Israel went ahead and the *Haganah* prepared with pitifully few weapons for the conflict that was to come.

Israel's superb air force had humble beginnings, when the only aircraft available to the *Haganah* were old basic trainers such as this Polish-designed R.W.D.8.

1947: The War of Independence

The 1948 War of Independence was, in statistical terms, the bloodiest of the Middle East wars. But it was a war that had to be won lest the infant state of Israel was crushed before it had even been born. Using improvised weapons and tactics, the few Israeli forces fought back at their Arab attackers and won against all the odds. Weapons came from various sources, but the men came from Jewish communities around the world and, though speaking many tongues, they were forged into the military David that defeated the Arab Goliath. They had one basic motivation – if they failed, they would be exterminated as a nation and as a people.

Left: From the very first, the existence of the state of Israel has depended upon the willingness of its citizens, both male and female, to fight and win against the odds. To the young *Haganah* volunteers in 1948, the war for survival was to be the first in a bitter series of conflicts.

Below: One of the very first aircraft types to equip the new Israeli air force was this Spitfire LF.Mk 9E, one of several assembled from spares and scrapped parts and flown by RAF veterans and local Jewish pilots.

From their point of view, the war that is now known to Israelis as the War of Independence had two distinct phases. The first phase was the period up to May 1948, when the state of Israel was proclaimed, and the second phase was the period of conflict that followed.

The first phase began in earnest during 1947. Up to that year the Jewish settlers in what was then known as Palestine had established themselves by migration and hard work into enclaves in what was still a predominantly Arab country. Their settlements were not welcomed by the resident Arabs and for many decades there had been between the two groups friction that had at times broken out into open conflict. The

Jewish settlers had organized themselves into what became the founder units of the present Israel Defence Forces, but these units were purely local in character and were poorly armed, trained and structured. Their successes were the result largely of the fact that their Arab opponents were even less well organized and armed. This situation began to change rapidly during and after 1945. The stream of Jewish immigrants from war-torn Europe into Palestine grew into a massive flood, much to the alarm of the Palestinian Arabs and the surrounding Arab nations, and gradually the latent hostility re-established itself as open warfare once more. There were ugly riots in the various towns and

cities, attacks were made on farms and outlying villages, and supply convoys were ambushed en route to the more remote Jewish communities.

These attacks were made in spite of a continuing British military presence, which remained in Palestine until the new state of Israel was established in May 1948. The British had the unenviable task of keeping a form of imposed peace between the Jews and the Arabs, and carried out their unwanted task with a somewhat unintended bias towards the Arabs, a bias imposed largely by political reasons not unconnected with Arab-dominated oil supplies. Thus Arab hostility and the counter-measures undertaken by the Jewish population were largely tempered by the police actions of the British. But the British could not be everywhere, and given their forthcoming withdrawal, during 1947 the hostilities became more open.

In many ways the conflict leading up to May 1948 was a form of guerrilla warfare. On both sides volunteer militia units were ready to defend what they regarded as their own territory, and trained and organized accordingly. On the Jewish side the Haganah and the various resistance and political groupings structured themselves more and more along established military lines with a formal chain of command, supply system and all the other trappings of military bodies. On the Arab side the organization was more fragmented, and although many volunteer fighters began to arrive on the scene from all over the Arab world they operated mainly as individual bodies operating in isolation. These bodies operated against Jewish interests and personnel inside Palestine itself, while their various agencies supplied funds and weapons from wherever they could. There were several of these Arab groups, typical being the Arab Liberation Army (ALA) which attracted some non-Arab recruits such as ex-German SS adventurers and British deserters, various youth organizations that attracted recruits from among the Palestinian Arabs themselves, and the Moslem Brotherhood based in Egypt. On the Jewish side there was the *Haganah* itself, the main Jewish 'national' military establishment, and the various Jewish resistance and self-defence units such as the Palmach, ETZEL and HIM.

The conflict begins

The British announced the forthcoming end of the British mandate in Palestine during February 1947. The United Nations Organization was supposed to take up the burden of determining a long-term solution to the establishment of a new Jewish state supposedly with an Arab element, but by the time such ideas were ready for implementation, the state of tension between Jew and Arab had extended beyond any rational solution: the various guerrilla and other military units on both sides had begun to fight one another openly. Across the various demarcation lines that sprang up, some well established by settlement boundaries and some imposed by the British military administration, there began a series of brief attacks, sniping and general guerrilla warfare. The British attempted to impose some measure of order between the two sides but such a task became increasingly difficult as the fighting increased in intensity. The Jewish agencies began to assume more of the responsibility for keeping their settlements and enclaves supplied, all manner of day-to-day requirements being transported in convoy fashion through areas that were predominantly Arab and therefore hostile. This led to a series of small-scale actions that came to be known as the 'Battle of the Roads'. The early convoys were often ambushed or turned back to the major towns by Arab groups, to the extent that the convoys were provided with armed guards to get through. These guards became more important as the Arab attacks and ambushes grew heavier, the Jews having to improvise armoured cars and armoured lorries, as well as specialized road-

clearing vehicles. The Battle of the Roads continued up to Israeli independence (and beyond in some areas) and provided nascent Israel Defence Forces with valuable experience of kinds that ranged from combat tactics to logistics.

Throughout the period up to May 1948 the Jews were poorly armed, largely with small arms from a variety of national sources. There were few enough of these weapons, and other than improvised vehicles there was no armour, no artillery and only a small number of mortars. Even this small arsenal could not be used openly, for while they remained the British did their best to prevent arms being carried or transported. Further supplies from abroad were strictly limited and had to be smuggled into the country. On paper the Jews had some 45,000 men and women ready to fight, but the general standard of training was poor and there were not enough weapons to supply all of them. On the Arab side there was a far greater number of combatants, both actual and potential, but although many of the Arab groups had weapons to hand their organization remained fragmented.

By early 1948 bombings and other attacks in Jewish areas grew in number, while sniping and other attacks increased in intensity. The Jews began to retaliate accordingly, and by early 1948 had carried out an internal reorganization that combined their various military forces into six brigades. More arms became available, mainly from Czechoslovakia, and the weapons that began to arrive included not only numbers of small arms but even combat aircraft. These were Avia S 199s (a re-engined Messerschmitt Bf 109), a type at best obsolescent but better than the handful of unarmed light aircraft that was all the Jewish air arm had to hand at the time. The numbers of aircraft were tiny, but were gradually supplemented by a few Supermarine Spitfires, and more aircraft had yet to come.

When the British announced that they were to withdraw from Palestine in May 1948, the newly organized *Haganah* began to make its defence plans. High on its

26 April 1948, and the first *Haganah* convoy travels the newly re-opened road between Tel Aviv and Jerusalem. Blockaded within the Holy City, 100,000 Jews awaited the food, medicines and other supplies in the convoy. Such was its importance that the armed *Haganah* escort consisted of 250 volunteers.

An Israeli air force Spitfire LF.Mk 9E, one of a batch of 50 previously flown by Czech pilots in RAF service. Some of these Spitfires were assembled from spares, but most were flown to Israel in September 1948.

list of priorities was the establishment of defended localities, where Jewish communities could undertake defensive operations. Jerusalem was such a location, but there the British military authorities attempted to keep the city under their control right up to their moment of departure. This was to have adverse consequences for the *Haganah*. Although these moves were supposed to be defensive in nature, they soon spilled over into aggressive ambushes and battalion-sized operations against the more heavily blockaded localities. Some of these actions grew into pitched battles that involved civilian casualties on both sides, and at times the Arabs were able to bring field artillery into play. The overall effect of these actions, known as Operation 'Daleth', was that the Jews stood ready to defend their most important areas and the Arabs suffered a series of defeats.

This positional jousting was not confined to the outlying areas: in coastal towns such as Haifa there was heavy street fighting, and the Jewish forces assumed control of the city. They were not so fortunate in Jaffa where British forces intervened. Elsewhere the local actions expanded into determined military campaigns and large areas of the country were cleared of the local Arab guerrilla groups. All these operations were undertaken by relatively small units, armed with little more than rifles and sub-machine guns, but even before Palestine had become Israel, it had become clear there was a total determination among the Jews to win: the spur was the realization that the Arab world was equally determined that a new Jewish nation would not be established in Palestine. The Jews therefore had no option but to fight. If they did not, they would cease to exist as a nation and as a people.

The second phase

With the establishment of the state of Israel in May 1948 the Jews became Israelis and a new period of the war arrived. Up to this time the Jews had been fighting the Palestinian Arabs, but from then onwards they were fighting the rest of the Arab world. The various Arab nations situated around the borders of the new Israel had originally hoped that the Arabs within the country would themselves have been able to defeat the aspirations of the new nation, but Operation 'Daleth' and other countermoves had prevented so easy a way out. The only alternative was to invade the new nation, but although the strengths of the combined Arab armies was overwhelming in numbers and firepower, Israel's Arab neighbours proved themselves surprisingly unwilling to make the necessary moves.

The most powerful of the Arab nations in organized strength was Jordan, which had the Arab Legion, a well-armed force established along British lines. Almost as powerful was Egypt, but its forces were less well armed and less well organized. The Iraqi forces to the north were equally strong, and many other Arab states deployed weapons and manpower for the forthcoming struggle. But for all this the forces the Arabs actually brought to bear were well below their potential strengths. As ever, the Arab governments failed to co-ordinate their moves or their timings. The two most powerful nations, Egypt and Jordan, failed completely to operate in accord, the result largely of deep-seated political differences between them, and consequently their power was considerably diminished.

On the Israeli side manpower was flocking to the new state to swell the numbers in the ranks, and arms purchases were making their benefits felt. The first fighter aircraft had arrived from Czechoslovakia, some ancient artillery had arrived from France, and three rusting corvettes had been taken over by the new Israeli navy. On the debit side the number of weapons was still well below that required even to arm the newly-established Israeli Defence Forces, and too many experienced men had been lost in the operations before independence. In general, training levels were well below those required by any military force, and there was not much time to organize and prepare.

Two factors aided the Israelis considerably. One was the determination of the Israelis to defend their territory. All around the borders of Israel small and poorly-armed local forces held off vastly superior forces for days and weeks, providing the commanders with precious time to prepare. There were many of these small actions, typical being one on the

The Israeli air force had at one time seven Boeing B-17Gs, three of which were flown from the USA, bombing Cairo on the way after refuelling and arming in Czechoslovakia. At this stage they had little armament or navigation equipment.

1947: The War of Independence

October 1948 saw Operation 'Yoav', in which Israel took advantage of Arab disunity to drive the Egyptians back through the Negev desert. Machine-gun armed Jeep units played a prominent part, scouting and raiding most effectively.

approaches to Tel Aviv, where a garrison of 70 armed only with small-arms held off an Egyptian brigade for six days before withdrawing.

The other factor was the poorly co-ordinated and badly directed nature of Arab operations. If the Arab Legion had attacked across Israel to the sea in the early days it could easily have cut the nation in two as there was little to stop it. Instead, the Legion moved against Jerusalem and in the consequent close-quarter fighting took the centre of Old Jerusalem but lost the bulk of its combat potential in the process. To the north the Iraqis managed to take a sizable chunk of territory, but combined Syrian and Lebanese attacks succeeded in taking only a small strip of border territory. These border actions were largely local in character, for the Arabs were unwilling to commit large numbers to their invasion and the small Israeli forces were equally unable to defend every metre of their borders. But the Israelis did attempt to retake Jerusalem, being repulsed only at the last moment with heavy casualties, many of which were inflicted upon the elite *Palmach* units.

Away to the south the expected Egyptian attacks proved to be surprisingly tentative, and were largely halted by an air strike on 29 May which stopped their forces only 23 miles (37 km) from Tel Aviv; the Egyptians then settled down to establish a defensive line, thereafter showing little inclination to proceed further. This suited the Israelis very well at the time, for following its action in Jerusalem the Arab Legion managed to advance as far as Latrun, once again threatening Tel Aviv and cutting the main route to Jerusalem. There the Legion was held by desperate Israeli attacks that caused heavy casualties on both sides.

By this time the United Nations had arrived on the scene and a truce was declared on 11 June. It was welcomed on both sides. The Israelis badly needed time to organize, to prepare new units and to rearm. The Arabs were equally ready for a rest: their early dreams of rapid conquest had been shattered, and with those dreams went the last hopes of any unified command structure or conduct of operations. From June 1948 onwards the Arab forces operated in virtual isolation from one another, thus enabling the small Israeli forces to concentrate on them one at a time.

In the air the small Israeli air force had been able to make its mark in several actions, providing air strikes and some local defence, but it was unable to prevent several night attacks on Tel Aviv by the Egyptian air force. The tiny Israeli navy was also in action at this time. The three corvettes pressed into action had once been refugee transports impounded by the British at Haifa, but once in Israeli hands they were armed with light field guns lashed to their decks, and thereafter patrolled the coastline to prevent the Egyptian navy taking any offensive action. The port of Tyre to the north had been shelled, and this tiny force was to do much more in the months to come.

The imposed truce did not last long. By early July the Israelis had reorganized themselves sufficiently to launch offensive operations, using strike forces up to four or five brigades strong. One of these four-brigade strike forces was used in Operation 'Dani', an attempt to clear the Arab Legion from the Latrun area. This objective was not achieved, but the route to Jerusalem was cleared and the Arab Legion was forced out of the centres of Lod and Ramleh. Farther to the north another brigade took Nazareth, and Syrian and Lebanese counterattacks were defeated, partly by air strikes carried out by the Israeli air force, which was growing in power and effectiveness with every mission. Once again there was heavy fighting in the Jerusalem area, the Israelis being prevented from retaking the Old City by stubborn Arab defenders manning the ancient walls of the city.

Once again an imposed truce was called, and by mid-July the Israelis were once more regrouping. Their first armour had arrived during June and was prepared for action. In retrospect this armour was not much, being only a handful of elderly and obsolete ex-French H-35 light tanks, but other tanks such as two Comets and a few Shermans had come the way of the Israelis via some dubious supply channels. These tanks had seen limited action during Operation 'Dani', but at the time their combat effectiveness was limited. The same could not be said of a mechanized commando unit (led by one Moshe Dayan), whose success presaged future tactical events. This commando was made up of a number of Jeeps, improvised armoured cars and captured anti-tank guns, and was used in a highly aggressive manner during the recapture of Lod. Armed with machine-guns, the Jeeps were used in small numbers to scout and raid, and produced effects far out of proportion to their numbers.

In the air the number of aircraft was increasing as well. More aircraft had arrived, including a batch of four North American P-51 Mustangs smuggled out of

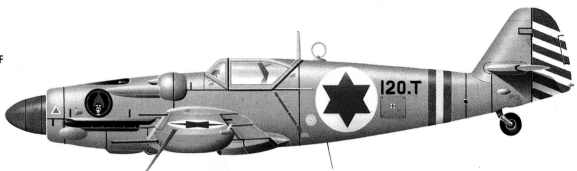

One of 25 ex-Czech air force Avia S.199s supplied to Israel from May 1948 onwards. Powered by Jumo 21-F engines, they formed the bulk of Israel's defences for some while.

the United States, and Douglas C-47 Dakota and other transport aircraft were also procured. A small force of three Boeing B-17 Flying Fortresses was also obtained, and this was soon put to use for nuisance night raids on the Arab capitals of Damascus and Cairo. These raids caused little damage but made a great impression on morale, both Arab and Israeli. Supermarine Spitfires were obtained from Egyptian wrecks and salvage dumps, and Bristol Beaufighters were flown out from the United Kingdom without official sanction.

Captured weapons

Many Israeli weapons came from captured stocks, and varied from armoured cars to artillery. The artillery was particularly welcome although many Israeli operations relied only on the use of mortars.

Throughout the July fighting the Egyptian forces were content to remain behind their defensive lines and stayed there throughout the period of truce that lasted until October 1948. They then made a few raids into Israeli territory, providing the Israelis with an opportunity to drive the Egyptians from the areas they occupied. The lack of any co-ordinated Arab policies enabled the Israelis to deploy no less than three brigades, their only tank battalion and what little artillery they could muster to undertake Operation 'Yoav'. This drove the Egyptians back through the Negev desert and cut off a sizable Egyptian force at Faluja, where it remained until the end of the war. The United Nations once more imposed a truce on 22 October, but on that very day the remaining forces of the Arab Liberation Army attacked a settlement near the Lebanese border which gave rise to the counter-operation designated Operation 'Hiram'. This was a rapid campaign that lasted only three days, but in that time the Arab Liberation Army was virtually wiped out and the Syrians and Lebanese defeated to the point where an area of Lebanon up to the Litani river was occupied by the Israelis.

The conduct of Operation 'Hiram' was repeated during late December when Operation 'Horev' was conducted against the Egyptians in the Negev. By the time these two operations were carried out, the Israelis

had increased in strength and effectiveness to a high degree in comparison with the period immediately after independence. Israeli confidence improved by leaps and bounds, and led by young commanders with no hidebound concepts of tactical niceties the Israelis broke all the established rules of warfare, attacking as and when they thought fit and in the places where they were least expected. Using fast-moving columns of armed Jeeps, White scout cars and armoured cars they hit their enemies time and again in a manner that produced dramatic results with relatively few casualties to themselves. Most of the weapons used were light but the attacks were pressed home with a determination that increased their effective firepower. This was particularly noticeable during Operation 'Horev', when raiding columns of armed Jeeps moved into the Egyptian rear areas and created havoc while another force moved up and down the Egyptians' immediate front. With the enemy's attention diverted, another column had moved through the mountains inland and outflanked the main Egyptian positions. Within days the Israelis were deep in the Egyptian Sinai and had captured the important Egyptian base at El Arish. The Egyptians were saved from total destruction by the unexpected intervention of the United Kingdom, which invoked a 1936 treaty and threatened to aid the Egyptians. The Israelis could not take on such a large external power and they had to be content with an armistice signed with Egypt on 11 January 1949.

With the Egyptians out of the running, the Arab world had lost one of its strongest participants, but the other Arab states still declined to sign any armistice or treaties themselves. They remained implacable as ever but had to content themselves with watching the United Nations draw up the future boundaries of Israel. These boundaries were occupied during the early months of 1949 and involved a series of Israeli operations to ensure that the Arab forces withdrew where necessary. The largest of these operations was Operation 'Uvdah', when an Israeli column advanced across the Gulf of Eilat to Aqaba to take possession of the outlet to the Red Sea. During this advance the Jordanian Arab Legion threatened to take some form of action but in the event did not do so. Both sides had suffered enough losses for the new boundaries, and wished to prepare for what both sides knew would be a future conflict.

By mid-1949 armistice had been signed between Israel and all the involved Arab states other then Iraq. The costs of the war had been high. In terms of equipment and weapons the Arabs had lost heavily and in the process swelled the meagre Israeli arsenals considerably. The cost in Arab lives has never been finally established but it must have run into many thousands. The Arab and Palestinian refugee problem that has bedevilled the Middle East ever since had begun, and the seeds of future conflicts had been sown in a fruitful soil. For the Israelis the cost was considerable, for at least 6,000 had been lost, about one in every hundred of the population. But the new nation had been established by a race only just starting to recover from the holocaust in Europe. In the process the Israelis discovered that when they had to fight for their existence they did so with a determination and talent for the task that was to establish them as one of the most remarkable military nations ever to emerge.

Jewish settlers working on the land were vulnerable to guerrilla attack, and *Haganah* members often took their turn guarding against such occurrences. In the orange groves at Rehovoth, such vigilance was essential following large-scale Arab infiltration.

1956:The Suez War

During the Suez incident Israel carried out a lightning campaign against Egypt in order to obtain various territory and access concessions, while France and Britain sought to regain their hold on the Suez Canal. The operations ended in a climb-down for the French and British, but the Israelis obtained all they required at very low cost in casualties and equipment. The exercise was a test of mobilization procedures and the capabilities of the growing air force and its new jet equipment; at the same time the old aircraft of the War of Independence were once more put into action. The Egyptians were soundly beaten, but world opinion demanded an all-round withdrawal and the Israelis relinquished their newly-won territories. The entire campaign took just over 100 hours and was a portent of what the Israeli armed forces could achieve.

Left: The early Israeli army mobile columns relied heavily on armed Jeeps and scout cars such as this example armed with ex-German (and probably ex-Czech) MG 34s.

Below: The Israeli navy frigate *Mitvach* which was based at Eilat along with her sister vessel, the *Miznach*.

By the mid-1950s the Middle East had settled down, outwardly at least, to a period of relative calm. But these appearances were deceptive. The main centre of power in the Arab world had become Egypt, which was moving increasingly into the Soviet sphere of influence with all its attendant economic and military aid benefits, to the point where Egypt was the most powerful of all the Arab nations and the principal potential enemy of Israel. This enmity had become

apparent in the Gaza Strip, a thin tongue of Egyptian territory protruding along the coast into Israeli territory along the Sinai border. This strip had become one of the most populated areas of that part of the world, and apart from being a military area was a location for numerous refugee camps that housed the Fedayeen, an increasingly militant grouping of Palestinian bodies that sought to use guerrilla tactics against the Israelis to regain their lost lands. Throughout the early 1950s

The infant Heyl Ha'Avir obtained aircraft from many sources, some of them illegal. Several de Havilland Mosquitoes were bought to provide real muscle, and this is an FB.Mk 6 bought from France at a knockdown price. After 1952, several became unglued in the air and only a handful remained to see service in the 1956 war.

these groupings became increasingly active as their camps became training grounds of political unrest and combat tactics. Raids against Israeli border posts and other installations became commonplace, and many of these guerrilla operations were condoned if not actively assisted by Egyptian aid and weapons.

Israel was not the only nation aggrieved by the emerging power of Egypt. To the west the various Algerian freedom fighters engaged in their prolonged war with the French settlers were receiving active Egyptian aid of all kinds. If this was not enough in itself, France and Israel had already forged some common links, especially in the years after 1952 when France was the only nation willing to supply Israel with modern weapons; even before that some French politicians had been active in the supply of weapons, especially the old H-35 tanks, in the early days of independence.

Thus France was already on bad terms with Egypt when Colonel Nasser seized from the UK and France the Suez Canal and all its associated company assets in July 1957. The United Kingdom was deeply involved in the Suez Canal and its links to the Persian Gulf, and it was not long before the British and French began to contemplate armed military intervention of some kind. It was a situation in which the Israelis soon became involved, for apart from the Fedayeen the increasing air power of the Soviet-supplied Egyptian air force was becoming a major threat to Israel. A combined operation against Egyptian bases would be a good opportunity to nullify this threat, and after secret meetings with France and the United Kingdom Israel began to prepare war plans. In strategic terms the Israelis were

to provide an excuse for French and British intervention by carrying out an airborne landing close to the Suez Canal Zone, and would thereafter attack through the Sinai and carry out air strikes against Egyptian air bases.

For Israel the main problem was whether or not the Israeli war machine was capable of carrying out the large-scale operation envisaged. By 1956 the Israeli armed forces had grown considerably from the levels of 1949, but the bulk of the personnel were scattered throughout Israeli society as reservists. These would

By 1956 the Israeli army used increasing numbers of ex-American half-tracks to carry the mechanized infantry units; this picture shows Israeli troops moving into the Sinai desert during the Suez operation.

Eleven Gloster Meteor F.Mk 8s were purchased in 1953 at a cost of £36,250 each. They formed the front line of air defence for Israel, and saw combat during the Suez campaign.

Israeli air force North American P-51D Mustangs were still in service in 1956 as a carry-over from the days of the War of Independence. They were used during the Suez operations for ground attacks in the Sinai Desert.

Israeli half-tracks towing 17-pdr anti-tank guns withdraw from Sinai in the El Arish area of the Gaza Strip during the latter period of the Suez operation.

During the Suez operations the P-51Ds of the Israeli air force were used to cut telephone communications in the Egyptian Sinai, and thus were effective in isolating some of the Egyptian garrison units.

closed to shipping because of the Egyptian guns based along the gulf.

The international operation was scheduled to begin on 29 October 1956, by which time it was apparent to all the world that the French and British were planning to carry out some form of offensive operations. For the operation Israel assembled an armoured brigade, two mechanized brigades, six infantry brigades and an elite paratroop brigade. In typical Israeli fashion the brigade commanders were provided with a considerable degree of freedom to carry out their operations. The Israeli air force assembled about 150 aircraft (about 100 of them jets) for the operation, and further support was to be provided by two French squadrons based in Israel. French support was also provided for the Israeli navy, which would otherwise have been outnumbered by the stronger Egyptian navy.

Operation 'Kadesh' began on the afternoon of 29 October with some communications-cutting air strikes followed by the dropping of a small paratroop force near the back of the Mitla Pass. The rest of the paratroop brigade, mounted in half-tracks and supported by a light tank squadron using French AMX-13 tanks, overran a defended position and moved 190 miles (305 km) across the Sinai desert to join up with their comrades the following day. This action was typical of the dash with which the remainder of the 'Kadesh' force was to operate over the next few days. The reservists had started to mobilize on 26 October, and it was not long before the first formations were moving up to their battle positions. The mobilization went far more smoothly than had been expected and some units

have to be mobilized and sent to their units in a dauntingly short time, and once in action had to prove their combat worth. But all the same preparations for Operation 'Kadesh' went ahead with three main aims. One was the destruction of the Fedayeen bases in the Egyptian-held Gaza Strip; then followed the destruction of the Egyptian bases in the Sinai; and as a long-term objective there was the seizure of the Gulf of Aqaba approaches to allow Israeli shipping to use the port of Eilat. Although this port formed part of the border settlement of 1949 it had remained virtually

found themselves with far more men than they had dared expect.

On the night of 29 October a brigade captured the Egyptian position at El Quseima which meant that after only a few hours of combat they were in a position to outflank the main Egyptian positions in a group of static positions known as the 'Triangle'. These positions were 'hedgehogs' surrounded by obstacles and containing heavily defended positions that used armour either as static artillery or at best as a form of reserve. In strength

these Egyptian forces comprised six strengthened infantry brigades together with artillery and some armour, but tactically they were static in character. This factor showed itself to be the decisive one when on the morning of 30 October a reconnaissance unit found that a pass leading to the rear of the Abu Ageila defences had been left open, allowing one of the armoured brigades to move against this important position from the rear. The results can well be imagined, but frontal attacks by two other brigades

Israeli army troops advance into the Sinai during the Suez operation. At that time the Israelis were still using a great deal of ex-British equipment and uniforms, including Sten guns and British webbing equipment.

By 1956 few of the ex-Czech Avia S.199 fighters remained in front line service, but a small number were still in use in the reserve and were called upon to provide back-up defence aircraft.

During the Suez campaign two Boeing B-17G Flying Fortresses were used to carry out night nuisance raids on Cairo and other Egyptian cities.

Two Israeli air force Boeing B-17G bombers were still in service in 1956 but were used only for night bombing raids, at which they proved highly effective and had an inordinate effect on Arab morale.

One of the biggest Israeli navy prizes during the Suez campaign was the capture of the Egyptian destroyer *Abrahim el Awal,* seen here being towed towards Haifa after an Egyptian raid on that city.

were far less successful. These two brigade attacks were against Um Katef, and were stopped in their tracks. Both commanders were replaced (one of them was killed in the attack anyway) and the units were thereafter more successful.

In the air the Israeli air force soon gained air superiority and thereafter indulged not only in attacks on the Sinai air bases but in direct support of the ground battles. This support in one case took an unexpected turn on 31 October as two battalion combat teams moved towards the Jebel Libni area to ambush an Egyptian armoured column moving up into the area: the column was intercepted by the Israeli air force, which completely halted it. With that force out of the way the road to Ismailia was open to the Israelis. To the north and south, meanwhile, the Israeli columns fought their way through the defended Egyptian localities. El Arish fell once more to Israeli troops on 1 November, and thus in only a few days the Israelis had achieved all their objectives in the Sinai.

1956: The Suez War

Following the Suez campaign Israeli forces withdrew from Sinai. Here Israeli half-tracks towing 25-pdr gun-howitzers pass through a check point near El Arish and back into Israel.

With Sinai won the Israelis turned their attentions to the Gaza Strip, but already events elsewhere were taking their toll. The French and British forces moved in to the Suez Canal zone on 31 October and called upon the Egyptians and Israelis to withdraw to a distance of 10 miles (16 km) on each side of the canal to permit them to occupy the area. The forewarned Israelis complied, but the remaining Egyptians had to be driven back. The Egyptian navy attempted to intervene in events by shelling Haifa, but during this mission an Egyptian destroyer was intercepted by a combined French and Israeli naval force and subsequently captured. Israeli paratroop units dropped directly onto Egyptian air bases and destroyed them, and an amphibious landing took the last Egyptian defences at Ras Nasrani.

Israeli troops in Gaza after the capture of the town. Seen in this picture are White scout cars, half-tracks, Sherman tanks, Jeeps and ex-American 2½-ton trucks.

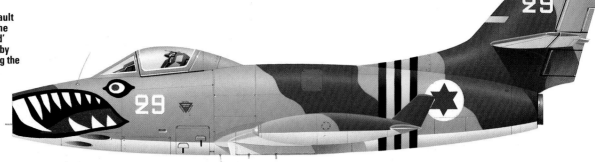

One of the Israeli air force Dassault M.D.450 Ouragans used during the Suez campaign sports the 'Allied' recognition stripes also carried by French and British aircraft during the operation.

By 5 November it was all over. The Anglo-French amphibious operations around the Canal were successful enough, but a withdrawal was soon enforced by the incensed weight of world opinion. The Soviets threatened to intervene directly and the Americans held out the threat of all manner of economic and military sanctions if the two nations did not withdraw. This they did, and Israel was also forced to withdraw from the newly conquered territories. Israeli forces started to draw back to Israel on 9 November, destroying roads and installations as they went. The subsequent political arrangements established the right of Israel to obtain access to the port of Eilat and the final Israeli war objective appeared assured.

Thus the Suez affair ended as far as the Israelis were concerned. Their reservist army had manage a remarkable series of victories, and in a seemingly free and easy manner the commanders had used their forces in a tactical way that would not have been contemplated in many other armies. The brigade commanders had taken advantage of every opportunity offered, and lower down the command chain unit commanders displayed a flair and determination unexpected in a citizen army. The actual combat time had only just exceeded 100 hours. During that time the Israelis suffered casualties of 172 dead and 700 wounded. They had lost four prisoners of war but took 5,581. Again the exact number of Egyptian casualties was not released, but they must have been in the tens of thousands. Perhaps the greatest effect of the Suez campaign was that it proved to the Israelis that their reservist army could function in a full-scale campaign, but in the short term they were the happy recipients of vast mounds of war booty of all kinds, much of this matériel ending up in their own stockpiles for the future.

Fleet Air Arm Sea Hawk FB.Mk 3s on HMS *Albion* during the Suez campaign. These aircraft attacked Egyptian air bases and carried out numerous missions over the Egyptian mainland.

Israeli troops stand guard as a batch of Egyptian prisoners-of-war shuffle to captivity. During the Suez campaign the Israelis took 5,581 prisoners for a loss of four POWs of their own.

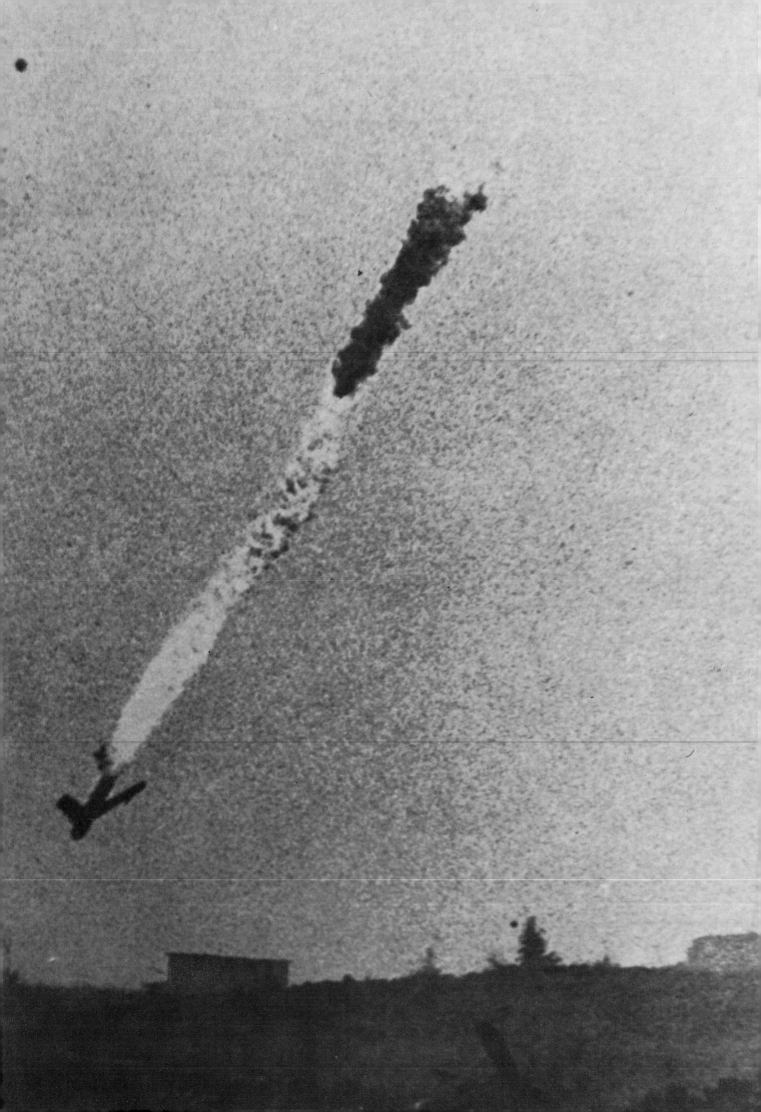

1967:The Six Day War

The 1967 Six Day War was one of the most remarkable conflicts in history. In a few short days the Israeli armed forces took on the might of the Arab world, and won. It was a war of movement by large armoured formations using forceful and free-moving tactics that constantly kept the Arabs off guard and on the static defensive, where they could be easily immobilized. But this war of movement demanded air superiority and that was obtained by a classic example of the pre-emptive first strike, made by the entire Israeli air force.

Left: An Egyptian MiG-17 plunges to earth following a hit in the tailpipe from an Israeli heat-seeking missile, probably a Sidewinder. Few Egyptian aircraft were able to operate following the devastating Israeli pre-emptive strike.

Below: The Six Day War was destined to become one of the classic examples of the effectiveness of modern armoured warfare. The expanses of the open Sinai desert made possible the use of large armoured formations.

In mid-1967 war clouds were once again gathering over the land of Israel. The Egyptian and Syrian armies were mobilizing, and Egypt was strengthening her land forces already in position in Sinai. To the north Syria had also mobilized a good proportion of her armed force and even Jordan was preparing for conflict. From all over the Arab world contingents of troops were arriving in the border states surrounding Israel. During May Israel too carried out a mobilization of the Israeli Defence Forces and settled down to see what would happen. For once Israel had time to carry out the mobilization at a steady pace, and there was time to prepare weapons and equipment for what was to

come. For the Israeli leaders the question was whether to wait for the Arabs to attack or to strike first.

The seeds of the forthcoming war were sown in the days following the 1956 Suez affair. Despite the Arab defeats the Soviet Union re-established its influence in Egypt and within a few years had set up political, economic and military agreements with nearly all the Arab nations in the areas surrounding Israel. There followed the usual largesse of weapons and equipment to all who asked, and it was not long before nations like Syria and Egypt had weapons in service that were well in advance of anything the Israelis could field. Some of this equipment was so modern that it was in Arab use

1967: The Six Day War

long before the Soviet and other Warsaw pact armed forces had been supplied. With the equipment came the advisers who gradually permeated all aspects of Arab military doctrine and military thought to the extent that troop dispositions and tactics were identical to those used by the Red Army.

If the renewed strength of the Arab armed forces were not enough for the Israelis to endure, there was also the added problem of the Arab guerrillas. For years after 1957 the guerrillas continued their attacks on the border areas of Israel, steadily organizing themselves into groups supplied with Soviet-produced weapons and other equipment. Their attacks grew in scope and scale until the groups were conducting virtual open warfare using support from the various Arab armed forces. This support at times included artillery and rocket fire, and in the years leading up to the 1967 war artillery fire ranged all over the Israeli hinterland from batteries situated on the Golan Heights and directed by Syrian gunners. This artillery fire not only made life in the settlements under the Golan almost impossible but drove home the point that large tracts of Israel were open to long-range artillery fire. The imposed borders that dated back to 1949 rendered large areas of Israel open to the possibility that a sudden attack would be able to drive a corridor from the Arab states to the sea. From the Golan to Haifa is only 32 miles (50 km), but farther south the borders imposed in 1949 meant that from the annexed territories west of the River Jordan to the sea there was a corridor only 9 miles (15 km) wide. These West Bank territories had been annexed by Jordan in 1950, and although Jordan was one of the least hostile of all the Arab nations towards Israel the political situations meant that the Kingdom of Jordan had to remain allied to the Arab cause. The proximity of Arab territory to the sea meant that artillery could at any time be brought to bear against the coastal towns and cities such as the crowded industrial areas of Tel Aviv.

Thus in 1967 the Israeli had their choice to make. In typical Israeli fashion they decided to strike first: their defence forces were mobilized and ready, their contingency plans were prepared, and the mood of the people was such that for a short while political considerations were laid aside. As always the situation was

that the Arab forces were close at hand in overwhelming numbers and with more weapons and more firepower. The Israelis were fully mobilized, but their inferior numerical strength was such that to carry out full-scale campaigns on all fronts was impossible. Their plans were to attack the strongest Arab forces first, carrying out defensive measures against the others until Egypt had been defeated. This meant holding the line against Syria in the north while the attack was launched in the south. It was hoped that Jordan would refrain from joining in, but just in case she did a reserve unit was placed near Jerusalem to hold any possible advances.

It was just in time. At the beginning of June 1967 the Egyptians closed the Straits of Tiran to Israeli shipping, thereby shutting off the port of Eilat. This openly hostile act provided the Israelis with the reason they required to start hostilities.

The 1967 war can be regarded as taking place on

By 1967 the ex-American Sherman tank was hardly recognizable when compared to the World War II original. A new and longer 76-mm (3-in) gun had been fitted, the suspension had been updated, and much new stowage had been added.

An Israeli air force Nord 2501 Noratlas drops supplies, a measure that was sometimes used during the 1967 Sinai operation to keep forward columns moving when deep in the desert.

One of the most important Israeli aircraft in service during 1967 was the Dassault Mirage IIICJ, which was used both for air defence and for ground attack using bombs and rockets.

The few Egyptian MiG-17F 'Fresco-C' aircraft that survived the initial Israeli strike could make little impression on the course of the campaign and were used mainly for ground attacks; they proved to be no match for the Mirage IIIs in air combat.

After the Six Day War more and newer equipment was supplied to the Israelis from the United States, including numbers of Bell UH-1 Iroquois troop-carrying helicopters.

three fronts and these will be considered one by one. The main action took place in the south against Egypt, and it was here that the greatest successes were achieved.

The Sinai campaign

The war against Egypt opened with a pre-emptive air strike. This had long been the main purpose of the Israeli air force, which had practised long and hard the tactics it would employ. The air strike was delivered early in the morning of 5 June 1967 and lasted about three hours. Some 200 aircraft took part in the series of strikes made against nine of the major Egyptian air bases (four in Sinai, three near the Suez Canal and two near Cairo). The attacks were delivered from low level and much of the destruction was caused by cannon and machine-gun fire. Some bombs were used, including the 'concrete dibber' bombs that wrecked runways and were seized upon by the world's media as a new Israeli 'secret weapon', but the effect was that by the end of the attacks the Israeli air force had destroyed 286 Egyptian aircraft and had made the much-vaunted Egyptian air force virtually useless as a short-term weapon. The Egyptians were not the only ones to suffer. Attacks against Syrian, Iraqi and Jordanian air bases again produced a tally of destroyed aircraft, and by the end of the day the Israelis had gained the air supremacy they were not to lose in the days that followed, at a cost of only 19 Israeli aircraft. Thereafter the Israeli air force could concentrate on air support for the ground forces, and it was not long before they were busy in that role.

The ground war in the Sinai soon became one of the classics of armoured warfare. On the Egyptian side there were at least seven divisions deployed ready for an attack into Israel, supported by massed artillery and

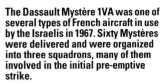

The Dassault Mystère 1VA was one of several types of French aircraft in use by the Israelis in 1967. Sixty Mystères were delivered and were organized into three squadrons, many of them involved in the initial pre-emptive strike.

at least 1,100 tanks and self-propelled guns. To be used against this array of military might the Israelis had three divisional task forces, or *ugdot*, variable in strength and size but consisting in the main of armoured and mechanized brigades. A brigade stood ready to isolate the Gaza Strip and a paratroop brigade was ready for use as a mobile reserve. There were also several combined armour-infantry combat groups with support or other specific roles.

The Egyptian forces were deployed along Soviet lines with a concentration in the usual 'triangle' Rafah–El Arish–Um Katef. In the Gaza Strip a division stood ready to be cut off by any moves the Israelis made, and a second Egyptian line was disposed south from El Arish to the centre of Sinai. The main Egyptian scheme was that these two lines would hold any Israeli attack until two armoured divisions could move into counter-attack positions. On paper this looked good, but as in 1967 the Egyptian forces were emplaced in mainly static positions, and once battle had been joined they tended to assume the classic 'hedgehog' positions that cost them so dear in 1957. Also, the carefully-laid Egyptian plans were often nullified by poor communications, by units in the wrong place at the wrong time, and by general confusion.

The Dassault Mirage IIICJ was widely used in 1967 and has since become an important component of the Israeli air force. It has been used as the basis for the highly-successful Kfir fighter-bomber.

All that was left of four Egyptian air force MiG-21F 'Fishbed-Cs' at the Abu Sueir air base, a scene that was repeated at nearly all the other Egyptian air bases following the initial Israeli air strike.

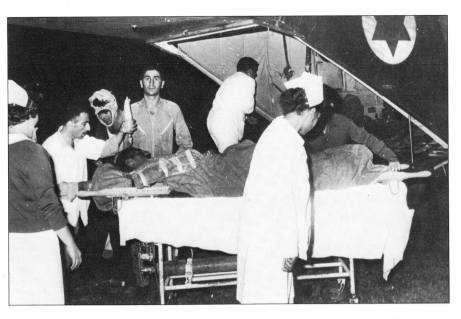

Following the Six Day War an Egyptian missile boat sank the Israeli destroyer *Eilat* on 21 October 1967. Here casualties from the action are carried on to an Aérospatiale Frelon of the Israeli air force.

One of the most effective tanks in use during the Six Day War was the British Centurion. Armed with a 105-mm main gun, it proved very reliable and able to withstand battle damage thanks to its thick armour.

The three divisional *ugdots* of the Israeli force each had its own specific task to perform. The northern *ugdot* had to smash its way through the strong Rafah position and move along the coast to El Arish. To the south the southern *ugdot* was to take the Um Kalef positions. The central *ugdot* then had to move between the two positions ready for the big breakthrough and the subsequent armoured battles that could be expected in central Sinai. While all this was in progress another force would move far to the south to Sharm el Sheik at the extreme tip of the Straits of Tiran.

The Israeli attack started on the morning of 5 June. In the north the Rafah positions fell and the leading units of the *ugdot* were in El Arish by midnight. The taking of the Gaza Strip was delayed by the need to overcome fortified positions, but by the middle of 6 June it too had

fallen. The taking of the Rafah positions had opened the rest of the Egyptian defence line to further attacks. To the south the Um Kalef positions were finally taken in a night attack, and the road to the centre of Sinai and its passes was now open. The central *ugdot* was also able to move into position on time and by then all was ready for the expected Egyptian counterattacks.

These materialized right on time. One was virtually ambushed, being taken in the flank by an Israeli tank brigade while the hull-down tanks of another Israeli tank brigade prevented it from advancing. This action took place near Bir Lahfen, while another counterattack near Abu Ageila never even got under way and was destroyed. Thus the Egyptians lost the cutting edge of their countermoves even before the expected battles in Sinai. In these armour battles the Israelis used Centurions and Patton tanks against the Egyptian T-54s and T-55s. On paper the Egyptians should have been able to gain the upper hand, but the tactics of the Israeli units coupled with the close air support provided by the Israeli air force overwhelmed them. The Egyptian tank crews were often tied to carefully drilled tactics and when in doubt usually assumed a defensive posture. The Israeli tank crews consistently attacked and used their initiative when any opportunity presented itself, and thus maintained their edge over their opponents. Their tank gunnery was better too.

On the morning of 6 June the two northern *ugdot* joined forces and raced towards the Mitla and Giddi Passes. In their way there were still considerable Egyptian forces, but these were considerably fragmented. A series of running battles developed during which the Israelis maintained their advance, and by the evening of 7 June the Israelis were in the Mitla Pass: with the pass sealed the remaining Egyptian armour was then bottled up in the approaches as it tried to retreat to the west. The area then turned into a terrible stage of destruction. The Israeli tanks holding the pass destroyed all that came near them while the Israeli air

force bombed and strafed the Egyptian columns until the area was a scene of carnage and destroyed equipment.

The carnage continued on 8 June, and on that day all Egyptian resistance collapsed. The Israelis reached the Suez Canal at El Qantara in the north, Ismailia in the centre and Suez in the south. In the Sinai desert whole units abandoned their vehicles and weapons to move off across the desert in a desperate attempt to reach the canal. Thousands never completed the journey and perished in the deserts. They left behind them mountains of weapons and all types of equipment that ranged from chemical warfare clothing to complete SA-2 'Guideline' surface-to-air missile batteries.

The Jordan campaign

It had been hoped in Israel that the strong armed forces of Jordan would make no attempt to take part in the war, but this was not to be. The Kingdom of Jordan was by 1967 under a great deal of Egyptian influence, to the extent that the army was controlled by an Egyptian general and two Egyptian commando battalions had been moved into Latrun on the eve of the war. When the Arabs declared the forthcoming conflict to be a *jehad* (holy war), Jordan had no option but to join in and on 5 June Jordanian artillery opened fire on Israeli air force bases, and some shells landed in the outskirts of Tel Aviv.

The Jordanian air force made some attacks but was

After the Six Day War the Israelis occupied the banks of the Suez Canal and its associated lakes, and used this patrol boat armed with 0.5-in (12.7-mm) machine-guns to police these areas.

The Sherman tanks still in service in 1967 were mainly used against the Jordanian and Syrian borders, and were usually manned by reservist units. They were still able to give a good account of themselves due to the tactics employed by their crews.

Many Sikorsky S-58 helicopters were used during the 1967 campaign in Sinai to make rapid troop and supply movements, and maintain the momentum through the Egyptian defence positions.

soon neutralized by the Israeli air force, fresh from its successes against the Egyptian bases. However, the Jordanian army was a different proposition. Along the border it had seven infantry divisions in well fortified positions, and two armoured brigades with M47 tanks were not far away. The Israelis had only reserve units along the same border, and many of these were local territorial units. There were few tanks to hand, and many of those that were available were of the old Sherman (updated) type. Some reserve units intended for use on the Egyptian front were re-directed to the Jordan border once the Israeli high command had decided to attack the Jordanian positions before the Jordanians could launch their own attack.

The campaign against Jordan was a highly improvized affair. There was none of the long-term planning that marked the war against Egypt, and units were rushed into action as and when they became available. In the event the attack was made by two brigade-sized *ugdots* and the focus of the attacks was Jerusalem. The main attacks took place on 6 June and were surprisingly successful in spite of the disparity in numbers. The Israeli successes were compounded by a series of rushed Jordanian armoured counterattacks, but these were countered by Israeli armour emplaced hull-down in perfect defensive positions to combine with Israeli air force strikes. It was during these counter-attacks that Jordanian morale started to break, and thereafter Jordan's opposition started to crumble.

Around Jerusalem the fighting was more of an infantry affair and took the form of defensive positions stormed in hand-to-hand fighting. Tanks could not move into the narrow streets and aircraft could not attack the confined areas involved. Gradually the

Israelis moved house-by-house towards the Old City until they were confronted, as in 1948, by the ancient walls. Here a handful of defenders could hold off large numbers and it was not until a half-track crashed through the Lion Gate that the Israelis could enter the Old City. Once they were inside the remaining defenders left, and the Western Wall (all that remains of the Temple of biblical times) was in Jewish hands for the first time in 1,900 years. It was one of the high spots of the whole war for the Israelis.

Outside the Old City there was little left of the Jordanian army on the west bank of the Jordan, and when scattered units tried to take a stand they were destroyed by the Israeli air force. The Israelis were soon standing on the shores of the River Jordan with the entire West Bank in their hands. Although the road to Amman was open, the Israeli units had strict orders not to cross the Jordan so the war against Jordan was all over by 8 June.

The Syrian campaign

If the campaign against Egypt was the most spectacularly successful, the campaign against Syria was undoubtedly the most hard-fought. It was also a campaign during which, in the initial stages, the Syrians did exactly what the Israelis wanted them to. As the attack against the Egyptians started on 5 June Arab entreaties were made to the Syrians to open some form of offensive in the north to divert at least part of the Israeli strength. Instead the Syrians did nothing. They remained in their positions and confined their efforts to the usual artillery fire and air strikes. In retaliation the Israeli air force virtually decimated the Syrian air force in a rapid series of counterstrikes. This further per-

A burning Egyptian T-54/55 tank, typical of many that met their end at the hands of the well-trained Israeli tank crews, who once again demonstrated a talent for the requirements of tank warfare.

suaded the Syrians to remain where they were and, apart from a few tentative forays that were beaten back by Israeli local defence units, they continued to do nothing.

This lack of action from the Syrians was even more surprising considering that it was their action in carrying on the artillery bombardment of the border areas and fostering the various actions of the guerrillas in Syria and Jordan that had largely caused the 1967 war. By then Syria was the home of a large number of Palestinian resistance and guerrilla units who continually harried Israeli settlements along the borders and carried out a programme of terrorist actions against Jewish interests around the world. Throughout the days of the campaign in the Sinai the Syrians did next to nothing, and by 9 June the Israelis were in a position to contemplate their future actions. What they wanted was to clear the Syrians from the Golan Heights and press them back to positions where their artillery could no longer dominate the plains below.

It was a formidable objective. The Golan Heights rise sheer from the plains along almost the entire length of the northern border of Israel, and the Syrians were well established along the heights. Along the crest of the heights, nearly 1,000 ft (305 m) above sea level, Syria's Soviet advisers had established three defensive infantry lines which were well sited, defended with masses of artillery and anti-tank guns, and in many places by concrete blockhouses. Manning the forward defences were three infantry brigades with, farther to the rear and acting as a form of mobile reserve, no less then three armoured brigades plus another five mechanized infantry brigades. These units were liberally supplied with tanks of all kinds and were covered by an umbrella of about 200 anti-aircraft guns.

The bulk of the Israeli units deployed against the Syrian positions had at least a part of their strength deployed in Sinai. For as long as the Sinai campaign lasted the Israelis were content to assume a defensive stance against the Syrians, and the fact that the Syrians did nothing from 5 to 9 June was distinctly in Israel's favour. When operations against the Golan were ordered the commander there had at his disposal about 20,000 men and about 200 tanks, mostly elements of eight brigades (three armoured, four infantry and one paratroop). The size of the front meant that only about one-third of these units could be used in any attack.

The plan was to attack simultaneously at several points. The main attack was to be where the Syrians least expected it, in the north where the escarpment was the steepest and the Syrian dispositions correspondingly the weakest. The attack was made on 9 June, and at five main points the attack was mounted by combined infantry and armour while to the south of the line a combined tank and paratroop operation was carried out against the southern Golan. It was a hard slog. The Israeli tanks and infantry had to fight their way up the almost sheer slopes against the well-entrenched Syrian lines, and casualties were high. At one point 35 tanks started the operation but only two reached the crest. In places special engineer vehicles had to clear a path for the tanks. The attacks were supported by close strikes from the Israeli air force in spite of the heavy anti-aircraft defences. During these support missions the air force lost some 40 aircraft but maintained its support missions until it was too dark to operate. By that time some toeholds had been gained on the crest, and some of the many concrete bunkers had been eliminated with napalm.

As darkness fell the attacks died away. The night was spent in moving up fresh units and holding off a number of disjointed counterattacks. As dawn broke the attacks started again and it was not long before the Syrian resolve cracked. In many units officers simply left their units and moved to the rear. Their abandoned units then broke and ran, leaving the Israelis in com-

The Six-Day Tank War

Although assisted by pre-emptive and continuous air strikes, Israel's tank crews had nonetheless the awesome task of fighting on three fronts against the enormous combined might of many Arab armies. Using courage, skill, improvisation and guts, they turned and routed their enemies and enacted one of the most spectacular victories ever seen in the history of tank warfare.

1 An Israeli Sherman fights its way up to the Golan plateau against dug-in Syrian T-34 tanks.

Israeli advance

1st day
2nd day
3rd day
4th day
5th day
6th day
☆ major tank battle

LEBANON

Damascus

Massada
Kuneitra
Boutmiye

Haifa
Tiberias

SYRIA

Jenin
Tubas
Tel Aviv
Nablus
Damiya Bridge
Amman
Jerusalem
Bethlehem
Jericho

Gaza
Rafah Khan Yunus
El Arish

ISRAEL

Abu Agheila
Kusseima

JORDAN

Bir Hassana

Suez

Nakhl

Taba

Sinai Peninsula

Abu Zenimeh

EGYPT

SAUDI ARABIA

2 Israeli Sherman tanks have suffered heavy casualties inflicted by Jordanian Pattons positioned in olive groves. When the Israeli force retreats to regroup, the Pattons break cover and follow, a running battle ensues and a narrow victory for Israel results.

3 Israeli Centurions advance through the Ismailia Pass, which is strongly defended by dug-in T-54 tanks. The Centurions with their heavier armour move forward in the centre, while Israeli Pattons, which are lighter and more manoeuvrable over soft sand, rush around the rear of the defenders.

The carnage of the Mitla Pass after 8 June 1967. Visible are a T-34/85 tank, an SU-100 assault gun and T-54/55 tanks. The rest of the vehicles are ex-Warsaw Pact trucks of several types.

mand of the heights. The subsequent pursuit took the Israelis right across the mountains and onto the road to Damascus. Behind them the Syrians left tanks, artillery and piles of equipment that later were pressed into Israeli use.

The Israeli advance was halted about 32 miles (50 km) from Damascus by the intervention of the United Nations, which announced a cease fire. To prevent possible conflict with the Soviet Union the Israelis moved back about 12 miles (20 km). The Golan Heights were in their hands and the threat of the guns that once dominated the plains had been lifted.

The entire campaign against Syria had lasted 27 hours.

The war at sea

Compared with the land war, the war at sea was comparatively low key. The Israelis had only the Egyptian navy to face, but as this was numerically far superior to the tiny Israeli naval arm the Israelis had no choice but to assume their usual stance and attack. This they did in their usual style by carrying out offensive raids on Alexandria harbour where Israeli frogmen caused some damage while surface raiders inflicted even more. In material terms these early raids achieved little but they did put the Egyptians onto the defensive and generally unsettled them. At sea Israeli destroyers encountered a force of Egyptian sub-marines and in the subsequent flurry of action at least one submarine came off the worse. Otherwise in the Mediterranean Sea there was little naval activity other than the standing Israeli patrols.

On the Red Sea there was more action. Based at Eilat at the end of the Gulf of Aqaba was a small force of Israeli motor torpedo boats. In one raid these small craft travelled the entire length of the gulf and captured Sharm el Sheik and were waiting to welcome the Israeli paratroops who later arrived in a full-scale helicopter assault. It must have been a surprise to find the navy there before them.

The 1967 war lasted from 5 to 10 June, and consequently it has gone down into military history as the Six Day War. It was ended only when the United Nations imposed yet another cease fire on the evening of 10 June, probably just in time. The Israelis were on the Suez Canal, had cleared the Jordanians from the West bank, and were over the Golan Heights and well along the road to Damascus. If they had advanced any farther there must have been some form of intervention from the Soviets or some other member of the large powers, with results that are now impossible to guess.

In orthodox warfare the usual ratio of attackers to defenders is generally considered to be at least three to one in the attackers' favour for any degree of success to result. During the Six Day War the odds of attackers to defenders was consistently the other way round, for

This camera-gun sequence shows a camouflaged Syrian MiG-21 being engaged by an Israeli fighter; it would appear that this 'kill' was made using cannon fire only. The combat was over the Golan Heights.

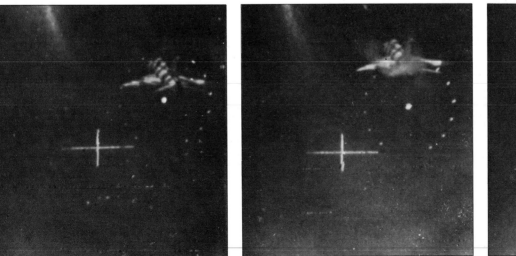

The smile of success: Moshe Dayan in Jerusalem following the victories of the Six Day War. Dayan was Minister of Defence during the period of the 1967 war, and was responsible for the overall conduct of the fighting.

the Arab armed forces outnumbered the Israelis in everything from manpower to weapon strengths and firepower. But it was the Israelis who attacked, and they attacked unaided; and they won a victory that will go down as one of the most remarkable in the history of warfare. In every case the Israelis fought just that much better. Despite the fact that their equipment and weapons were often not as modern as those of their opponent they used what they had in an aggressive and forthright manner.

This time, apart from the slight withdrawals along the approaches to Damascus towards more defensible positions, the Israelis held what territory they had taken. They also kept control of the battlefields together with all the war booty they contained. But once again there was no peace, and as the dust settled both sides started to prepare for the next round.

For the Israeli navy the Six Day War was a limited affair. These patrol boats at Ashod were used to raid Egyptian ports, with some success. In the background is the ill-fated destroyer *Eilat*.

1973: The Yom Kippur War

The year 1973 was a desperate one for the Israeli state. For once they had been caught on the defensive by a well-planned Arab onslaught that had been timed to attack both ends of Israel at the same time. Recovering from the initial surprise attacks, Israel fought back and made successful advances into Arab territories, culminating in the crossing of the Suez Canal and the taking of the Golan positions from the Syrians. Again the Arab world had been defeated, but the 1973 war was a close campaign and the Israelis came near to disaster. As it was, it cost them dear in casualties and equipment.

Left: During the Six Day War the Israelis had captured large numbers of ex-Soviet 240-mm BM-24 and other calibre rocket launchers.

Below: The Centurion tank is still one of the most important of all the Israeli tanks in service. In 1973 it proved its worth by being able to absorb no end of battle damage.

During the years following the Six Day War of 1967 the Israeli Defence Forces went through a period of heady self-esteem. They had taken on the might of all that the Arab world could put into the field, and against all the odds and the established rules of warfare had been victorious. This self esteem was not so completely overwhelming, however, that the Israelis came to ignore the facts that they had once again been unable to impose any form of peace onto their still-hostile neighbours, and that although they had under their control large areas of what had once been Arab territory they were still vulnerable to attack. And any attack that succeeded would mean the end of the state of Israel for all time. So despite all their victories, the men and women of Israel took their turn in the conscription routines, were trained and then stood ready as reservists in case the need for them arose. To arm, the Israeli government borrowed increasingly large sums to

1973: The Yom Kippur War

finance the purchase of more and more up-to-date weapons and other equipment, so keeping the qualitative balance in their favour even if the quantitative balance could not be managed.

For the air force this meant the purchase of McDonnell Douglas F-4 Phantoms, McDonnell Douglas A-4 Skyhawks and all the various weapons and other accessories that went with them. More tanks such as M48 Pattons were obtained, along with large numbers of American M113 armoured personnel carriers that began to supplement the large numbers of old half-tracks in service. TOW anti-tank missiles were on the shopping list as well, and there was the prospect of a new assault rifle for front-line units. Many other weapons were either in service or on the way, mainly from the United States, for in the years following 1967 Israel and the USA had come increasingly to work together, the USA becoming the virtual sponsor of the Israeli state. This situation had come about for a number of reasons, not the least of which had been the continuing dominance of the Soviet Union in nearly all of the Middle East. Following the heavy defeat of the Syrian forces in 1967 all the equipment and weapon losses had been made good by the Soviet Union in a very short time, and although the Soviets could do but little with the Syrian military organization in the short term it could and did dictate some sweeping long-term changes. These changes ranged right across the entire Syrian military structure from officer/lower rank relations via tactical dispositions and attitudes, to maintenance of complex military equipment. The same actions had been taken in Egypt, but there the re-equipment had been on an even grander scale. Everything from missiles to tanks had been handed out on a lavish scale, and the same alterations in attitudes and tactical approach had been attempted.

Soviet frustrations

In 1970 the Egyptian President Nasser died. His successor was Anwar Sadat, a man who had to make his mark on the Egyptian nation somehow, and for his long-term objective he chose the defeat of Israel. In this he was to be frustrated not only by the general standards of unreadiness of his armed forces but by the presence of large numbers of Soviet advisers who so permeated the entire Egyptian military structure that they could veto any particular move that Sadat wished to make. This was further reinforced by the fact that the Soviets could switch the supply of weapons on and off as and when they chose, and they threatened to do so during 1971. It was too much for Sadat, who in mid-1972

ordered the Soviet advisers to leave the country. Large numbers of them did leave, though some remained, but it was enough: Sadat could at last have a free hand to attack Israel.

Various individual nations and the United Nations itself attempted diplomatically to establish some form of lasting peace between the Arabs and Israel, but none had any success. Under the cover of these diplomatic peace moves Sadat prepared for 'his' war. At the time Syria and Egypt were in close political accord, and a concerted plan of action against Israel was for once seemingly possible. By early 1973 Egyptian and Syrian preparations were under way. This time it would be different.

On the Israeli side the nation continued its everyday life and attempted to evolve a way out of the economic difficulties that the years of defence spending had brought about. It was getting to the stage where even a training mobilization could cripple the state's economic life for long periods, and thus the mobilization exercises became less frequent. In military terms Israel was stronger than ever with over 300,000 combat

Egyptian air force Mil Mi-6 'Hook' giant transport helicopters fly past during a parade held in Cairo prior to the 1973 war. At the time these were the largest helicopters in the world.

Egyptian air force Sukhoi Su-7BM 'Fitters' take off from an Egyptian air base to take part in the air strike of 6 October 1973. These aircraft are primarily ground attack fighters, and would thus have been ideal for use against Israeli ground targets.

Among the new equipment supplied to Israel prior to 1973 were numbers of 8-in (203-mm) M110 self-propelled howitzers, seen here during a parade in Jerusalem. These howitzers have a range of 16800 m (15,362 yards).

An Egyptian air force MiG-21PF 'Fishbed-J' shows off over the River Nile area while armed with two AA-2 'Atoll' air-to-air missiles. These aircraft were a considerable improvement over the early MiG-21s of the 1967 war.

troops, 2,000 tanks of all kinds, 900 pieces of artillery and over 550 combat aircraft. But a vital piece of the military infrastructure was missing, and that was the strategic intelligence which failed to see exactly what the Arabs in general, and the Egyptians in particular, were preparing. The Israelis somehow failed to note the Egyptian war preparations and were thus not well placed to defend themselves. It was not until the final stages of the Egyptian-Syrian moves that the impending conflict was seen as inevitable.

This lapse of an otherwise highly efficient intelligence organization led to the first line of Israeli defence along the Suez Canal becoming increasingly depopulated of personnel. The defences, set up along the east bank of the Canal, consisted of a line of concrete bunkers known as the Bar-Lev Line. When they were first constructed they were kept well up to strength, especially during the period up to 1970 when incidents along the canal were commonplace. These incidents varied from simple sniping to full scale air force opera-

1973: The Yom Kippur War

tions complete with dogfights and air strikes, and grew to such a scale that some Israeli references now know the period as the War of Attrition. But following an Egyptian-Israeli understanding during 1970 the defence lines along the canal were relegated more and more to the position of a quiet defence zone where the bunkers could be manned by reservist units for part of their annual reservist duty periods. Some of the bunkers were even closed down and others were held at only nominal strength.

The lack of activity along the canal was further encouraged by the building of a large sand rampart along the Egyptian side of the canal. This sand rampart was 100 ft (305 m) high in places, and although it proved the Egyptians with an excellent vantage point over the Israeli defences the Israelis did not object as the rampart was considered to be as crucial an obstacle to any large-scale crossing attempt by the Egyptians as it would be to the Israelis. What they did not consider was that the rampart acted as a perfect observation screen to hide the Egyptian preparation and build-up behind it. When the time came to make the actual crossing the ramparts were rapidly removed by the use of high-pressure water jets which removed the sand within a very short time ready for the large-scale water-crossing equipment to be put into position. Egyptian preparations for this crossing were typical of their entire plan of operations. The canal crossings were to be made at the same time as a massed armoured attack across the Golan by the Syrian army.

The attack was scheduled for 6 October, and its initial success was considerably assisted by two factors. One was that the day had been chosen specifically because it was the Day of Atonement (*Yom Kippur*) in Israel, one of the most important dates in the Jewish religious calendar when the life of the nation would be at a virtual standstill. The second factor occurred during the early part of 1973. Repeated Syrian and Egyptian moves gave the impression that an attack on Israel was imminent and a partial mobilization was called in Israel. Nothing happened, but the economic life of the nation was considerably disrupted for no apparent reason, so when September came around and the same apparent Syrian and Egyptian moves were noticed once more there was an understandable reluctance to call out the reserves once again. It was not until the first days of October that it was noted that Syrian tank unit moves were not just the usual unit rotation and replacement measures but that the new units were bolstering the units already in place. Indications came from Egypt that large-scale troop movements were in progress, but it was not until 5 October that the first mobilization measures were taken. The Israeli air force acted independently and went for a full mobilization but for the army it was already too late. The usual procedure of reservists reporting to mobilization centres where they were formed into brigades before moving forward was simply abandoned. As personnel arrived they were formed into hasty small units and moved forward.

The attacks came on 6 October. The Egyptians crossed the canal and the Syrians began a massed armoured attack towards the Golan. The progress of the conflict, which lasted for three desperate weeks, can best be followed by describing what happened on each front, but on both fronts there were three distinct phases. These were Israel's defence, her containing countermoves and the final counterattacks.

The Israeli defence

In Sinai the attacks over the canal started with a series of air strikes against radar installations, air bases and the Bar-Lev Line itself. These were quickly followed by the actual crossing of the Suez Canal. The high sand ramparts were duly demolished as planned by the high-pressure water jets and the amphibious crossing was made in assault boats in typical Soviet

style. In fact the whole Egyptian army attack was carried out using typical Soviet 'steamroller' tactics in a carefully planned sequence according to a strict timetable. In this type of warfare the Egyptian soldiers excelled, but if at any point the timetable could not be followed, or if something went wrong, it was noticeable that the command structure allowed for very little local improvisation or flexibility. The result was often confusion and muddle, to the extent that although the initial Egyptian objectives of two crossings to gain two large

Top: Soviet-designed K-61 tracked amphibious cargo carriers of the Egyptian army parade through Cairo carrying Unimog trucks prior to the 1973 war.

Above: PMP ribbon bridge pontoons are carried through Cairo on KrAZ-255B trucks. It was the use of these rapidly-deployed bridging pontoons that enabled the Egyptian army to cross the Suez Canal in a very short time and surprise the Israelis.

bridgeheads on the Sinai side were attained, the overall objective of reaching the important supply roads that ran north and south through Sinai and parallel to the canal was not achieved.

For the Israelis the Bar-Lev Line was supposed to act as a form of trip wire to allow time for covering armour farther back to move forward into carefully pre-prepared emplacements to provide defensive fire. This plan did not work for the simple reason that there were not enough men and tanks in the area to carry it

out. The entire Bar-Lev Line was manned by only 456 men with only about seven tanks anywhere near the defensive positions. Instead of falling back from their bunker positions many soldiers chose to remain where they were and to fight it out. Many were overwhelmed but others held out for several days, and one position in the far north (the 'BudaPest' bunker) managed to hold out for the duration of the entire war.

As the Israeli armour rolled forward towards its prepared defensive positions it was countered by a nasty

A well-weathered Israeli army Centurion tank captured by the Egyptian army shows signs of the battle in which it was taken. The fenders and stowage boxes have been penetrated by small-calibre shot and some of the stand-off armour side plates are missing.

Left: A clip from a cine camera sequence as an Egyptian air force MiG-21PG 'Fishbed-J' rolls in for an attack on Israeli ground positions in the Sinai during the initial stages of the 1973 war.

This Israeli air force Agusta-Bell AB. 205 helicopter was brought down by an Arab SA-7 'Grail' heat-seeking missile. These shoulder-fired missiles proved very effective against slow-moving targets, but were less effective against high-speed aircraft.

1973: The Yom Kippur War

surprise. The first waves of assault infantry to cross the Suez Canal took with them what appeared to be large suitcases. These suitcases contained the small but very effective AT-3 'Sagger' anti-tank missiles. These missiles were Soviet in origin, and being wire-guided they could be steered accurately at their targets. The result was that the first Israeli armour forays were met by a storm of missiles, many tanks being knocked out almost as soon as they appeared. The same applied to the early forays of the Israeli air force. As the Egyptians moved forward they moved under a screen of Soviet anti-aircraft radar and guided missiles that proved to be unaffected by what electronic countermeasures (ECM) the Israelis were able to employ. Wherever Israeli aircraft appeared they were met by a hail of guided missiles of all kinds, though the most feared anti-aircraft weapons proved to be the quadruple 23-mm cannon of the ZSU-23-4 self-propelled anti-aircraft weapon systems. These radar-guided weapons proved lethal to the Israeli aircraft and it was not long before the Israeli air force was suffering insupportable casualties.

By nightfall the Egyptians were over the canal in two bridgeheads with another smaller crossing near Suez to the south also proving successful. On the night of 6/7 October an Egyptian helicopter assault was made by several commando units near Baluza. These attacks were not a great success, although some of the commandos did manage to remain in action for a few days. In that same night Israeli armoured units started to arrive near the bridgeheads and pressed forward in a series of disjointed attacks that often stalled against

the Egyptian missile screen or against armoured units fresh from their canal crossing. Once again Israeli casualties were heavy, but the attacks had the effect of putting their opponents on their defensive guard and gained precious time for the main units to arrive from across the Sinai. As Israeli tanks arrived they were pushed straight into the attack in typical Israeli fashion, but all too often these early holding attacks were conducted without preparation, artillery support or infantry co-operation. Throughout 7 October these attacks continued and any Egyptian advances were met with fire from whatever forces could be mustered.

It was enough. By 8 October the worst was over as the forward and main elements of two armoured divisions arrived, one to be deployed near El Qantara and the other as cover for the important passes into the centre of Sinai. Although the Egyptians later denied the fact, these passes were among the Egyptians' initial objectives, though the dramatic defensive and holding attacks held them off. But the casualty toll was very high. Some Israeli armoured brigades virtually ceased to exist but with the two fresh armoured divisions in place the position was at least stabilized for the moment.

On the Syrian front the scale of the expected attack was finally recognized by the early days of October, and the crack 7th Armoured Brigade (one of the Israeli 'regular' armoured formations) was moved to the area. It was a move that saved the day, for when the Syrian attack opened on the afternoon of 6 October the tanks of the 7th Armoured Brigade were ready. The Syrian

During the Yom Kippur war the Arabs stunned the Israeli air force with a vast array of new surface-to-air missiles and guns. The Israelis soon evolved tactics and equipment to counter this barrage, but it was to be a very costly lesson.

Advancing infantry carried man-portable SA-7 heat-seeking missiles, and these took out some low-flying aircraft within 2-3 km by homing in on their exhausts.

A SA-2 'Guideline' medium-range surface-to-air missile site in the Egyptian desert, with a camouflaged 'Fan Song' control radar situated in the centre of a ring of six missiles (only five can be seen here).

Longer-ranged SA-2 and SA-3 missiles protected Egyptian troops as they crossed the Canal. Fired from their permanent sites, the SA-3s were used at low-level targets at 30-km range, while the SA-2s fired at high-flying aircraft at longer range.

SA-6s climb slowly from a shallow angle but reach a speed of 3200 km/h. Israeli planes could fly at the oncoming SA-6 in an effort to outmanoeuvre its constant tracking control equipment, but such positioning brought them within range of the SA-7 and ZSU-23-4.

Batteries of deadly ZSU-23-4 radar-controlled anti-aircraft guns opened up on incoming targets at up to 2 km. Each of these four-barrelled guns could put up 200 23-mm rounds in a 3.5-second burst, producing a barrier of explosive or armour-piercing shells through which few aircraft could penetrate and survive.

attack also followed the usual Soviet 'steamroller' methods, for it was launched by three mechanized divisions and two armoured divisions. The units defending the Israeli positions were thus vastly out-numbered but they were ready and alert, unlike the positions along the Suez Canal. The Syrians did not therefore have things all their own way as they had expected, but it was a very close-run battle in which tanks were knocked out by the hundred.

The defensive battle carried out by the Israelis was to become another classic of its kind. Despite the huge disparity in numbers and weapons involved, the superior defensive tactics of the Israelis paid hand-some dividends. The 7th Armoured Brigade managed to knock out no less than 300 Syrian tanks during the initial stages of the attacks, but to this brigade's south the much weaker 188th Brigade had to withstand a massed attack by 450 tanks with a tank strength of only 77 of its own. Using massed artillery fire and mobile anti-tank rocket teams, the Syrians ground the 188th Brigade out of existence and were accordingly able to move forward towards their objectives of the River Jordan bridges.

They were prevented from reaching the bridge by the intervention of the Israeli air force in a dramatic series of close-support air strikes against the Syrian columns. For this purpose all the units involved in the Sinai fighting were withdrawn, and once over the Golan they encountered massed guided-missile defences and yet more of the dreaded ZSU-23-4s. The Israeli casualties were heavy, but by a combination of air strike and skilled tactical use of whatever tank weapons or guns the Israelis were able to employ the Syrian tank columns were gradually ground to a halt. The Syrians' casulties were enormously heavy, it being later estimated that by the afternoon of 7 October they had lost no less than 600 tanks. But there seemed to be a never-ending stream of replacements, and their final thrust was halted only 6 miles (10 km) from one of the Jordan bridges by the arrival of fresh armoured divisions from the Israeli mobilization centres. By the

morning of 8 October there were three fresh armoured divisions in place. The 7th Armoured Brigade was still intact but the 188th had virtually disappeared. The defence had held.

The counter moves

By the third day the Syrian and Egyptian attacks had been held, and although Israeli ground had been lost, in neither the north nor the south had the attackers' objectives been reached. At the time this was not fully appreciated and for a while the Israeli cabinet even contemplated the use of nuclear weapons to hold the enemy. Fortunately this option was overruled and, following reports from both fronts, it was decided that

The Israeli air force still employs the McDonnell Douglas A-4E Skyhawk as an attack aircraft, and over the years has added to its electronic equipment. This Skyhawk stands ready for reloading; note the refuelling probe.

The cannon of a Skyhawk is reloaded with a fresh ammunition belt. This photograph clearly shows the underfuselage ordnance station loaded with three 1102-lb (500-kg) bombs and fuel tanks on the wing stations.

Above: An Israeli Centurion moves up into action during one of the first hurried armoured counter-attacks in the Sinai. These early counter-attacks were costly, but they purchased time to bring forward the main Israeli formations.

Above right: By 1973 Israel's little two-seat Fouga Magisters had been returned to the training role. In 1967 they had been used as ground attack aircraft to good effect, but by 1973 their role had been assumed by more modern aircraft.

The Israeli army has large numbers of M107 self-propelled guns that can fire a 147.2 lb (66.78 kg) HE shell to a range of 29,900 yards (32700 m). Enhanced ammunition has been developed with a longer range.

more conventional measures could still win the day. Counterattacks were ordered.

In the south the initial counterattacks were failures. They were launched, as had been the earlier holding attacks, without recourse to fire support or covering infantry and the brutal attempts to smash a way through to the Suez Canal foundered against the formidable Egyptian anti-tank screen. One Israeli armoured brigade virtually ceased to exist and by 10 October tank losses on the Sinai front were approaching 400. Many of these losses were later reclaimed when the battlefields were back in Israeli hands, many of them proving repairable, but that stage was still in the future and one immediate result of the stalled counterattacks

was that the local commander was replaced. The Egyptians continued to build up and consolidate their bridgeheads. By 9 October all the various bridgeheads along the length of the canal were combined into one line, but the line was not continuous. A distinct gap existed between the Egyptian 2nd Army to the north and the 3rd Army to the south. The gap existed just to the north of the Great Bitter Lake and was to have important consequences, for it was discovered by Israeli reconnaissance patrols and reported back to headquarters.

On the Syrian front the Israeli counterattacks commenced on the morning of 8 October. The Syrian defences proved resolute, but the attacks inched their

Dassault Mirage III

This Dassault Mirage IIICJ carries two Shafrir air-to-air missiles and supersonic external fuel tanks. This aircraft was widely used during the Yom Kippur war, and this example is proudly wearing 11 victory marks. Following the 1967 war, France imposed an arms embargo on Israel and it had to turn to America for arms, resulting in the procurement of the McDonnell Douglas F-4 Phantom. Following the arrival of these, the Mirage force became more involved in ground attack duties, and when replaced in this role by both Phantoms and Kfirs, took up training operations.

An Israeli air force Dassault Mirage IIICJ seen here armed with the Shafrir (Dragonfly) short-range infra-red seeking missile. The aircraft is French, but the missiles were designed and manufactured in Israel.

way forward and it was noticeable that the number of missiles being used was diminishing. The same applied to the anti-aircraft defences, and the Israeli air force was for the first time able to make partial use of the ECM equipment that had arrived literally the day before from American sources. Using these ECMs they were able to jam some of the guided missile radars, and although casualties continued they were nowhere near as severe as on previous days. As the use of the ECM devices increased the casualty rate went down accordingly. Away from the missile war the Syrian air force attempted to intervene but in the resultant air combats they suffered many losses, with no corresponding losses on the Israeli side after several encounters.

On the ground the Israeli attacks gradually forced the Syrians back until by 10 October they were in places back to the points from where the Syrian attacks had started. After the war it was discovered that the Syrian attacks had cost them no less than 867 tanks, some of them the very latest T-62s (the bulk of the Syrian armoured units were equipped with the T-54 and T-55, both of them with 100-mm/3.9-in guns, while the T-62 had an improved 115-mm/4.53-in gun; the Israeli tanks nearly all mounted a 105-mm/4.13-in gun). Added to this were thousands of other types of vehicle and other equipment of all kinds. The main difference between these counterattacks and the attacks made over much the same territory as in 1967 was that this time the Syrians, although defeated, did not run. Instead they held together and conducted their withdrawals with some skill.

By 10 October each side was beginning to feel the strain of several days of continuous combat. On both fronts some units had been in action ever since the conflict started on 6 October and were very tired. But more important on the Israeli side was that ammunition supplies of all kinds were getting low. Numerous aircraft had been lost and no replacements were at hand. Israel had had continually to plan for short campaigns,

and all the various logistic stockpiles had been arranged accordingly, but by 10 October these stockpiles were dangerously low. Ammunition expenditure, especially tank gun ammunition, had been far higher than anticipated but the Western nations proved reluctant to supply more for political reasons. However, the United States at least intervened and began to supply aircraft and other equipment. It was just as well, for the Egyptians and Syrians appeared to have no problems regarding supplies. The Soviet Union even supplied ground-to-air missiles direct from Red Army stockpiles while the war was still under way, the first time this course of action had ever been followed. At times the quantities of missiles available to the Syrians and Arabs appeared endless. On both fronts anti-aircraft and anti-tank missiles were fired in salvoes against individual targets to ensure a hit, with no regard to the cost of replacement.

The Israeli offensive

By 11 October the Israelis were once more ready to move back onto their preferred offensive. Their entire

A Dassault Mirage IIICJ armed with two Shafrir dogfighting missiles. Credited with a 75 per cent kill rate, these missiles use solid-state electronics and have been widely exported.

An Israeli air force Bell 205 in use in the casualty evacuation role. The Israeli armed forces rate the welfare of their wounded very highly, and take great trouble to get them to medical aid posts or hospitals as quickly as possible.

Action in the Sinai as a 160-mm Soltam mortar is loaded. Many of the Israeli mechanized formations use these heavy mortars in place of artillery, and some are carried on tracked vehicles.

military doctrine emphasized mobile warfare and the benefits of attack at all times, and at least they were ready. The offensive on the Syrian front should perhaps be given descriptive priority, for it was there that the first of the Israeli offensives took place.

The objective once the original Syrian lines had been reached was to break through towards the road to Damascus. This would force the Syrian forces back onto a defensive stance, meet the Iraqi armoured columns that were known to be moving south to join in the conflict and as a bonus it might dissuade the Jordanians from joining in with anything more than the token brigade sent rather reluctantly to join the Syrians. The Moroccans had also sent a brigade to the Syrian front but this brigade took the brunt of one of the earliest Israeli attacks and was consequently roughly handled. By 12 October the Israelis were well through the Syrian positions and advancing on Damascus. Some of their armoured units had managed to ambush the approaching Iraqi armoured columns and were able to knock out no less than 80 of them with no loss to their own number. In desperation the Syrian air force once more

attempted to wade into the battle under a screen of newly-arrived Soviet surface-to-air missiles, but in the resultant air-to-air combat they lost 29 aircraft.

On 13 October it was decided to call a halt with Israeli forces at their deepest point at a village named Sasa, about half-way between the 1967 cease-fire lines and Damascus. Although the breakthrough would have destroyed the remaining Syrian forces, it was not made for political as much as military reasons, only local consolidation of the Israeli lines being made before the usual United Nations cease-fire came into effect on 22 October. The only outstanding military operation during this latter period was a spirited infantry operation that regained the valuable surveillance point on Mount Hermon which had been lost during the early stages of the fighting.

It was afterwards estimated that in matériel terms the Syrians had lost 1,150 tanks during the campaign, the Iraqis about 100 and the small Jordanian force about 50. Nearly every Israeli tank was some sort of casualty at one time or another, but with Israel master of the battlefield many of these casualties were later recovered and repaired, only about 100 being total write-offs. To balance this were the large numbers of serviceable T-54s, T-55s and T-62s that had been captured and taken into Israeli service.

Away to the south in Sinai, Israeli commanders had been making contingency plans to mount a canal-crossing operation as early as 9 October. These plans envisaged the use of a special prefabricated bridge that was to be carried across the Sinai from Israel, and although this journey was started its progress was delayed, mainly by the fact that for some days to come Egyptians forces in the Sinai were far too strong to permit any crossing operations to be contemplated.

By 12 October it was apparent that despite the Israeli counterattacks the Egyptians were still determined to advance. Throughout that day signs that something big was imminent were reinforced by the reappearance of the Egyptian air force over Sinai, resulting in a series of running air-to-air combats. On the ground small probing attacks were undertaken and artillery fire grew in intensity. This Egyptian activity was carried out in response to Syrian requests for some form of diversion from the northern front, and on the morning of 14 October the big Egyptian attack was staged. It was a typical set-piece operation carried out with massed artillery fire from 1,000 guns, but as they moved for-

Infantry in the Golan take a break while the artillery lays down a barrage. Just visible through the smoke are two 155-mm (6.1-in) guns, and in the foreground is a command vehicle and map table.

1973: The Yom Kippur War

ward the Egyptians advanced straight into prepared defensive positions. Morover, as they advanced the Egyptians left the protective umbrella of their anti-aircraft defences.

About 1,000 Egyptian tanks took part in the operation and they were countered by about 700 Israeli tanks. It was the biggest tank battle since the 1943 Kursk tank battles and once again the Israelis demonstrated their superior tank gunnery. The tank guns were supported by TOW and SS-11 anti-tank missiles and by the air-to-ground rockets of the Israeli air force, which was able to operate for once without the bother of missile attacks. By the evening the Egyptian objective of Refidim was still far distant and the Egyptians had been well beaten. Their tank losses were later estimated to have been between 400 and 500; the Israelis lost six. All was ready for the canal crossing.

The operation to cross the Suez Canal was provided with the codename Operation 'Gazelle'. It was a difficult operation, for even as it was being undertaken there were still five divisions and 500 tanks of the Egyptian army on the east bank of the canal. The bulk of them were situated in static defensive positions, however, and thus proved to be of only limited value in the days to come. In their usual style the Israeli commanders chose to carry out the crossing where it was least expected, namely the point at which the gap between the two Egyptian armies that had been discovered some days previously. With the prefabricated bridge in tow and the usual panoply of assault engineer equipment in train, the crossing operation was undertaken on the night of 15/16 October.

The crossing itself proved to be a somewhat ill-organized affair. The initial crossing was made by paratroop units using amphibious boats but the planned prefabricated bridge could not be placed into position and a planned pontoon bridge never materialized. In the end the main crossing was made with improvised ferries that managed to get a few armoured

vehicles across by the morning. In the event the crossing met with virtually no opposition. The landings were made near a locality known as the Chinese Farm, and once the first units moved towards the east and north they ran into severe opposition. Any progress to the north was constantly frustrated, and no advance towards Ismailia past the road from Ismailia to Cairo was ever achieved.

With the initial crossing successful the bulk of the Israeli divisions could later cross using two new bridges. Attempts by Egyptian commandos to disrupt the crossings came to nothing, and men and matériel continued to pour over the bridges. But for all the masses of men and equipment that moved to the east bank it proved impossible to carry out the original

A 1102-lb (500-kg) bomb is loaded on to a wing station of a McDonnell Douglas A-4 Skyhawk. The censor has erased the tail marking for security reasons – yet another example of the Israeli obsession with all forms of internal security.

Advancing infantry travel towards the Golan heights in their half-tracks as an Israeli Skyhawk flies over at low level to demonstrate the close co-operation between air and ground elements of the Israeli forces.

An Israeli air force McDonnell Douglas F-4E Phantom flies off on an early-morning mission into the rising sun. The Phantom proved to be one of the main Israeli weapons of the 1973 war.

objective of turning north and cutting off the Egyptian 2nd Army from its supply networks. The Israelis were held south of Ismailia and there they stayed.

To the south it was different. The Israelis were able to move south across open country and even attempted an attack when they reached the outskirts of Suez. Here they over-reached themselves and were beaten back, but the Egyptian 3rd Army was still effectively cut off in Sinai. En route to Suez the Israelis managed to capture several Egyptian missile positions for later examination (and consequent countermeasure implementation) and the Suez to Cairo road was cut.

Thus the unfortunate Egyptian 3rd Army began to suffer, not only by the loss of military supplies but also by starvation and thirst. An Egyptian collapse seemed imminent but was prevented by the threat of Soviet intervention by several airborne divisions. This was avoided by a tacit recognition of the extent of their military expansion by the Israelis, and the same United Nations cease-fire that ended hostilities on the Syrian front was imposed on 24 Ocober.

Although the Egyptians were once more well beaten, as in 1967, this time they did not lose their military cohesion. Although the command and control structure did break down in many instances, the military units did not break up as they had done in 1967.

The 1973 war at sea

By 1973 the Israeli navy had grown substantially in numbers and skill compared with the navy of 1967 and

In what appears to be a hairy situation, an Israeli Mirage III rolls into an attack on an Arab surface-to-air missile (SAM) site. Such low-level flying was imposed by the effectiveness of the Arab electronic systems that the Israelis could not at first jam.

consisted of no less than 14 combat vessels. The Egyptian navy had also enlarged over the period and, with the usual Soviet advisers and supply of weapons and equipment, had grown into a far more formidable force than that which had been so out-manoeuvred in 1967. But in 1973 there was also the Syrian navy to face, and this too had a considerable combat potential. This potential had already shown itself back in 1967 when one of the 'Komar'-class fast attack craft of the Egyptian navy had sunk the Israeli destroyer *Eilat* with a Soviet-supplied 'Styx' anti-ship missile, an event that not only heralded a period of incidents that became known later as the War of Attrition but also heralded a new era in naval warfare.

The threat of the 'Styx'-armed vessels of the Egyptian navy was well appreciated by the Israelis, who were able to prepare for the next encounter by the introduction of new and elaborate electronic countermeasures and the introduction into service of their own Gabriel anti-ship missile. Combined with new evasions and other tactics the Israeli navy was well prepared for the war of 1973, and being a virtually 'all-regular' force with only a minimum of reservists to consider was actually placed on a high state of combat readiness as early as 1 October. By the morning of 6 October the entire force was either at sea or on an assigned combat station ready for action, and action was not long in coming. On the night of 6-7 October a task force operating off the

An Israeli navy missile boat at sea, with a coastal patrol craft on the left. The missile boat is of the 'Reshef' class and carries a mix of Gabriel and Harpoon ship-to-ship missiles.

The crew of an Israeli half-track watch as an aircraft bomb explodes in the distance. The weapon on the half-track is a twin 20-mm TCM-20 anti-aircraft system formed by fitting Oerlikon cannon on an old American mounting.

The Nesher is an Israeli copy of the Dassault Mirage 5J; about 100 were built by IAI, some in time to take part in the 1973 Yom Kippur War. The Nesher has an Israeli Atar 9C engine.

An Israeli missile boat fires a Gabriel anti-ship missile. The Gabriel has a warhead weighing some 600 lb (272 kg); a hit can easily sink a destroyer-sized warship and cause larger vessels extensive damage.

northern tip of the Mediterranean boundaries encountered a Syrian flotilla of three missile-armed craft and in a short but active combat session succeeded in sinking all three vessels. On that same night another Israeli force operating off the Egyptian coast encountered a force of torpedo boats and harried them back into Port Said. In an action on the following night intelligence reports guided an Israeli force towards a group of four missile-armed vessels, and in another short but sharp action three of them were sunk. In such consistently one-sided actions the Egyptians and Syrian navies were driven back into harbour where

they were unable to play any further part in the naval conflict. Even in harbour they were not safe for the Israelis once again managed to infiltrate commando units and frogmen into several Egyptian harbours, and in one such attack on Port Said were able to sink three vessels, one of them a missile-armed boat, inside the harbour with the vessels still at their mooring. Under such circumstances a force of Egyptian submarines grouped off the southern coast of Crete were unable to remain at sea and were forced to make their way back to their home bases without playing any part in the conflict. With its enemy driven from the sea the Israeli

navy was then able to patrol up and down the enemy coastlines at will.

Down in the Red Sea a small Israeli navy force was unable to break the blockade of the straits of Bab el Mandeh. They were not strong enough, and the straits were commanded by batteries of radar-controlled and Soviet-supplied 180-mm (7.09-in) coastal guns, but it did prove possible to operate even when the small Israeli vessels were within range of these guns for their evasive tactics and speed helped them to avoid the worst of the fire. Larger vessels would have had no chance though and the blockade remained intact throughout the war. Farther to the north, in the Gulf of Suez, the Israelis had a freer hand and did sterling service preventing Egyptian commando raids landing in Sinai, blockading and disrupting the ports of the Gulf and generally harrying the Egyptians.

The naval war of 1973 had no real impact on the main course of events in Sinai or on the Golan Heights, but if at any time the Egyptian or Syrian naval forces had been able to operate against the coastal towns and cities of Israel their impact could have been out of all proportions to their real effect, for the crowded built-up areas were not only the homes of the mass of the soldiers in the front line but also housed the bulk of the Israeli defence industries. As it was, it was the Egyptians and Syrians who had to suffer the harassment of attacks from the sea.

Conclusions

Although the world was thankfully not aware of the fact, the Yom Kippur War brought the globe to the brink of nuclear conflict. Apart from the contemplated use of Israel's own nuclear capability in the period immediately following the combined Arab attacks of 6 October, the world powers were also brought to the brink. It was the usual balance of power between the United States and the Soviet Union that was the main reason for the approach to nuclear war. Both states had interests in the region (the Soviet Union with the Arab states and the United States with Israel), but although the United States were initially unwilling to provide Israel with an open hand in the matter of weapon and ammunition supplies, the Soviet Union continued to

Above left: A camera sequence reveals an Arab MiG-21 'Fishbed' being destroyed by an Israeli missile. The lowest frame shows the missile hitting the aircraft's port wing to cause a fire that destroys the aircraft (top frame).

Above: During the Yom Kippur War an Israeli Phantom makes its final approach to its home airfield silhouetted against the early morning sky.

The Israeli air force had 12 of the large Aérospatiale SA 321 Super Frelon transport helicopters, and used them during the 1973 war to airlift troops into forward positions for raids or reinforcements.

The Kfir was an Israeli adaptation of the basic Mirage airframe to take an American J79 engine (intended for use in Phantoms). Later, foreplanes were added and the result is a first-rate ground attack fighter.

supply Syria throughout the period of conflict. Despite this investment the war went against the Arab nations to the extent where the total collapse of the Egyptian and Syrian armed forces seemed imminent. It was at this stage that the Soviet Union threatened armed intervention in the form of several full-scale airborne divisions. In return the United States also threatened intervention and put their strategic forces onto a higher state of alert. Thankfully the United Nations negotiations were fruitful and a cease-fire was imposed. Despite this there was still some sporadic fighting along the various cease-fire lines during the months to come, and as ever the Palestinian guerrilla groups did their best to take advantage of the situation and made some heavy raids into the villages of northern Israel. It was not until May 1974 that the final cease-fire agreement was signed with Syria; the corresponding agreement with Egypt had been signed in the previous November at the then-famous Kilometre 101 marker on the Suez–Cairo highway, and in time this led to another agreement in January 1974 whereby the Israeli evacuated their positions west of the Suez Canal and moved back to new positions some way east of the troublesome canal proper.

The 1973 Yom Kippur war badly shook the Israeli nation and armed forces. For all the previous Israeli victories, the combined Egyptian and Syrian attacks had caught the Israelis off balance and the subsequent fighting had cost them dear. The final casualty count was 2,412 dead, 508 missing and over 400 taken prisoner. (The correponding Arab tallies have never been officially released). In material terms the war had cost Israel the staggering sum of $2,200 million, the munitions stockpile was virtually exhausted and many weapons needed replacement. Perhaps the greatest effect was that Israeli morale took a severe knock while Egypt and Syria could both claim partial victories which considerably boosted the morale and self-confidence of the Arab world, a self-confidence that augured ill for the future of Israel.

It was true that at the end of the 1973 Israel occupied more territory than in October, but the cost was finally seen as being too high. The Israeli nation was unwilling to pay the price all the fighting had inflicted, and although the total casualties were well below those of the 1948 War of Independence, they were considered unbearable by the bulk of the nation. So once again the 'victory' of 1973 ended as yet another partial failure.

1982:The Road to Beirut

After many years of almost constant harassment by various Arab guerrilla groups against Israel's northern borders, the Israeli army moved into southern Lebanon in June 1982. There they remained, and an operation that was intended to provide 'Peace for Galilee' grew into a major military occupation of foreign soil. The operation started well enough, but with the advance to Beirut the character of the operation changed and the Israelis became bogged down in what became a civil war for Lebanon. Israel earned the displeasure of the world for the conduct of the fighting, and the results of the consequent ceasefire became a monstrous international problem.

Left: An Israeli M60 battle tank advances through Lebanon, well endowed with a layer of 'Blazer' active armour, which is designed to explode and snuff out the fire jet formed by hollow-charge anti-tank missiles.

Whereas F-15s and F-16s were used in the air superiority role over the skies of Lebanon, the main attack aircraft were Kfirs and F-4E Phantoms. Here a Kfir taxis to the take-off point, loaded with Mk 82 bombs and Shafrir/Sidewinder air-to-air missiles.

The years following 1973 saw a drastic reorganization of the Israeli armed forces. New equipment arrived to replace the losses of the Yom Kippur War, and the munition stockpiles were replenished. All manner of internal improvements were completed, among the most important being improved internal communications (roads etc.) to allow the rapid movement of forces from one front or area to another. Throughout the country local defences were improved to the point where settlements that once relied on a system of slit trenches and bunkers now took over concrete fortifications with such luxuries as emplaced tank turrets. The internal structures of the army and air force were over-hauled and some changes in tactical doctrines were introduced in an attempt to avoid any repetition of the worst blunders of 1973, such as the costly initial counterattacks in Sinai.

All this cost money, and the economy of Israel, never strong, went into a period of decline from which (at the time of writing) it has yet to emerge. Foreign aid, especially from the United States, was requested but was forthcoming only in limited amounts, and all the new weapons and equipment had to be purchased at market rates. Thus even the hallowed defence spending had to bear its share of the consequent finance cuts, though as yet these have had but little effect. The

1982: The Road to Beirut

Israeli army had by 1982 successfully carried out its programme of re-equipping the mechanized and armoured brigades. The Centurions were all given a thorough rebuild, new M48 Patton tanks were purchased from the United States and the infantry received new M113 armoured personnel carriers (the old half-track veterans were also given a drastic rebuild and issued to reserve units). Nearly all the towed artillery was replaced by new self-propelled pieces, again purchased from the United States. The Israeli air force gradually retired some of its older aircraft and purchased the very latest fighters such as the General Dynamics F-16 Fighting Falcon, but perhaps the greatest and most expensive investment was in sophisticated air-to-air missiles and advanced electronic countermeaures equipment. It was these electronic wonders that cost the state so dear, but they were soon to prove their worth.

Continuing harassment

Throughout the period following the cease-fire agreements of 1974 the Palestinian guerrilla groups continued their harassment of Israeli settlements and interest wherever they could. These harassments culminated in a series of airliner hijackings and a series of attacks on individuals and groups around the world, but closer to home the settlements near the border with Lebanon came under a prolonged series of attacks by rockets and mortar fire. The main group of guerrillas had by then long been established under the

common flag of the Palestinian Liberation Organization (PLO), into which the earlier *El Fatah* group was absorbed. Numerous small-scale counterstrikes were made against these guerrilla bands, some of which assumed the scale of small armies, but the guerrillas always operated along strict guerrilla warfare lines and many of the counterstrikes were thus either

Above: A Palestinian strongpoint captured by Israeli forces, with a Soviet-built DShK heavy machine-gun in its sandbagged emplacement. The DShK is a potent weapon, comparable to the M2 Browning.

One of the new Israeli air force McDonnell Douglas F-15A Eagles lands past troops manning an airfield surveillance radar system. Forty F-15s have been delivered to Israel for use as air defence interceptors.

The J79-engined IAI Kfir-C2 has proved to be an excellent multi-mission aircraft that can carry out ground attack missions and still act as a useful interceptor against aircraft such as the MiG-23 'Flogger'.

The canard foreplanes of the Kfir-C2 endow the aircraft with enhanced manoeuvrability for use in dogfighting and in the ground attack role. Here a Kfir is bombed up with a fresh load.

counterproductive or relative failures. These border attacks were compounded by terror bombings in most of the major centres of population in Israel, and the establishment of new settlements along the West Bank of the River Jordan added fuel to the tensions between Israeli and Arab.

Fighting in Lebanon

Into this unrest the problems of Lebanon intruded. After years of relative peace and co-existence, the various factions within Lebanon started to fight openly among themselves. Into this cauldron the Syrian army entered as a peace-keeping force, but in time this force turned into an army of occupation that gave rise to alarm within Israel. Not only did the Syrians occupy a nation that had for some time acted in a reasonably peaceful manner towards Israel, but it was also not long before the Syrians were aiding some of the more milit-ant Moslem Lebanese factions as well as providing

weapons and other support for the PLO, which was thus able to step up its activities against Israel from within Lebanon while at the same time it became involved in the internal Lebanese conflict between the Christian and Moslem factions.

It was the attacks on Israel that caused the first of the major Israeli incursions into the Lebanon in March 1978. This operation was carried out by about one-third of the strength of the 'regular' Israeli army covered by the air force. No reservists were involved although a few were called up to carry out some of the functions of the combatant troops back at their home bases. The 1978 operation was a straightforward advance as far as the Litani river, which was reached without much opposition. Once on the river, the Israelis began operations to root out any PLO units which might still be in the area, but as expected most of them had fled to the north.

By June 1982 the Israelis were ready to return to their

original border. At the time many observers expected the Litani operation to turn into a long-term occupation but this was apparently never the intention. Instead the Israelis chose to arm and organize some of the local Christian militias to keep the area clear of PLO activities. To add to these measures the United Nations imposed several contingents of peace-keeping forces into the area, but as time was to demonstrate their

activities were so restricted that their effectiveness was hopelessly limited.

The Litani river operation was made possible by one main factor, namely the peace agreement entered into with the old enemy Egypt. The Camp David agreements made peace between Israel and Egypt, but only at the cost of the Sinai territories. However, with Egypt peaceful Israel could concentrate more on the guer-

Below: The crew of a Centurion take it easy during a lull in the Lebanon campaign. This example is well loaded with extra stowage for the crew's kit and extra equipment including two roof machine-guns.

The Israelis have not had everything their own way during the Lebanon operations. This Israeli Phantom F-4E was shot down over the Bekaa Valley during July 1982 during a raid on Syrian missile bases.

Left: Deliveries of the General Dynamics F-16 Fighting Falcons to Israel have been marked by interruptions as the United States has sought to bring pressure on Israeli policies. The Lebanon campaign has caused several such delays in delivery of this potent fighter.

The 1983 excursion into Lebanon provided the IAI Python 3 air-to-air missile with its first action, and it is likely that several kills were claimed. These Kfirs carry a missile under each wing and, although they flew fighter missions over Lebanon, most of the kills fell to F-15s and F-16s.

rillas and against the far more implacable Syria.

The Litani operation was considered to be a partial success. About 300 PLO guerrillas were killed or captured, but the greatest effect was against the camps and supply dumps that sustained the groups. Perhaps the greatest surprise at the time was that the Syrians did not intervene, but in the months following the operation it was noticeable that the Syrian defences in

the Bekaa Valley were considerably strengthened. This was particularly true of the anti-aircraft defences, some of which were of the very latest Soviet types. If this were not enough, it was not long before the guerrillas were back as strong as ever. The United Nations troops were patently unable to prevent them infiltrating through the Christian militia areas, and at times the UN forces were pinned down inside their observation

The Merkava tank had its first operational trial during the initial stages of the advance into Lebanon, and proved to be an excellent main battle tank, with its 105-mm main gun capable of knocking out Syrian T-72 tanks.

posts by the crossfire between the PLO and militia.

The PLO attacks continued through 1980 and 1981 until some large-scale raids against schools and bombing attacks against transport centres inside Israel finally gave the Israelis the impetus to carry out some form of 'final' operation to clear the danger to the nation once and for all. At any one time the Israel armed forces had in their operational locker a number of contingency plans to meet all likely situations, and one

of these was adopted for the offensive known as Operation 'Peace for Galilee'. The operation was carefully planned well in advance by the use of such modern military aids as computers and especially the large and new Ground Tactical Training Centre (GTTC), held in a secret centre and used for training as well as operational planning. With this preparation the army was able to determine well in advance the likely scales of ammunition expenditure, POL requirements, ration

Below: The Lebanese campaign marked the operational debut of the IAI Kfir-C2, which was used mainly in the ground attack role. These Kfirs are armed with Sidewinder close-range dogfighting missiles under their wings.

Already sporting some 'kill' markings under the cockpit, this Israeli F-15 was used during the air operations over Beirut and over the Bekaa Valley against Syrian air force MiG-23 'Floggers'.

supplies and so on for the entire operation. Thus even such items as barbed wire were placed for prisoner of war cages when they were needed.

The operation began on 6 June 1982, and by 10 June the Israelis were on the outskirts of Beirut. The operation was carried out in the face of international condemnation, but the Israelis were determined to free their northern borders of the PLO menace and this time they did not stop at the Litani river. But before they could even reach this river they had to get past the PLO's initial lines of defence.

PLO organization

By 1982 the PLO operated as a guerrilla formation but in effect they had become a regular army with all the trappings of command, supply and administration of a regular force. They had even obtained supplies for such unguerrilla-like weaponry as heavy artillery and tanks, and north of the Lebanese border with Israel

were emplaced in such fixed installations as Beaufort Castle. Beaufort Castle dates from the time of the crusades, but for all that it was a formidable military obstacle on a commanding ridge overlooking the Lebanese coastal plain and the approaches to the north. If the Israelis wanted to move north they had to take that castle: despite the formidable physical obstacles to such an action they took the position with night attack. This night attack was a return to the old infantry tactics of the Israeli army. During the 1973 campaign the infantry had been used mainly in a support role, the main assault being entrusted to the armoured units. There was no way that armour could be used at Beaufort Castle, and the heights were taken in time-honoured style by a stealthy approach followed by hand-to-hand fighting. In military terms it was one of the sharpest and fiercest infantry operations in the Middle East for many years, but at the end of it the Israelis held the castle. The fighting took about eight hours, some of the fanatical PLO soldiers fighting to the

Below: During the advance to Beirut Israeli commando units carried out raids on Arab guerrilla camps near the coastline of northern Lebanon. These raids met with varying success, and some were undoubtedly repulsed.

last with a determination that surprised even the Israelis.

Beaufort Castle was not the only obstacle to progress. The Israeli air force would be needed to cover the advance but the Syrian guided missile batteries in the Bekaa Valley (some of them reportedly manned by Soviet personnel) would have hit any aircraft that ventured into Lebanese air space within range. To knock out this threat the Israelis employed their new and expensive electronic gadgetry. Starting by directing reconnaissance drones towards the Bekaa Valley, special aircraft used electronic monitoring devices to determine the frequencies and operational sequences used by the missile batteries; the drones themselves obtained some of this intelligence and transmitted it to receiver stations. With as much of this intelligence as they could gain the attack formations then moved into the Bekaa Valley. Carrying electronic devices to jam and counter the frequencies used by the radar and other homing devices used by the missile batteries, the attacking Phantoms and Skyhawks were able to destroy the batteries completely, and from then onwards operated unhindered by the Syrians' main anti-aircraft defences.

On the ground the Israeli columns moved rapidly north. In places they encountered Syrian defenders using tanks but in every case the Israelis' use of tactics and gunnery removed the obstacles from the scene. It was during this phase that the newly-supplied Syrian

Israel controlled the battlefield by using the Grumman E-2C Hawkeye airborne command and control aircraft.

T-72s with their powerful 125-mm (4.92-in) guns were encountered for the first time, but the equally new Israeli Merkava tank with the well-tried 105-mm (4.13-in) gun proved to be just as efficient as previous vehicles and also proved eminently suitable for the terrain over which it was operating. There was one hindrance that proved highly effective, however, and that was the anti-tank mine. On several occasions even simple explosive charges crammed into metal canisters proved capable of halting the entire advance for some time. In some areas the advance was made through built-up areas along single roads so if a lead tank was disabled it took time to shift it from the road and clear any further mines in the area.

By 10 June the Israelis were on the outskirts of Beirut. The bulk of the PLO, those who had not been bottled up in the coastal towns such as Tyre, retreated into the main built-up areas of Beirut and from there pro-

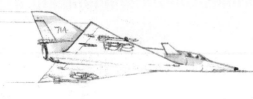

Once the Syrian radar units had been knocked out by Israeli Phantom attacks, IAI Kfir-C2s flew in with cluster bombs to wreck the SAM launchers.

War against the SAMs in the Bekaa Valley

In the Middle East conflict of 1973 Israel's air force had suffered heavy losses in the first few days of the campaign to the Egyptian and Syrian SAMs, but in the June 1982 invasion of Lebanon by Israeli forces the Syrian missile complex in the Bekaa Valley was destroyed without the loss of a single Israeli aircraft.

The Syrian air-defence complex in the Bekaa Valley consisted of two SA-2 batteries, two SA-3 batteries and some 15 SA-6 batteries, and had been in position for about 12 months before the Israelis carried out their attack on 9 June. The position of the batteries and their associated equipment had been closely monitored by Israel using RPVs equipped with electro-optical sensors which relayed the data to ground stations in the rear for immediate analysis. It soon became apparent to Israel that with a few exceptions the SAM batteries were static for extended periods and that their exact position could easily be determined.

There were four main parts to the successful attack on the SAM defences in the Bekaa Valley; electronic warfare, deception, attack of the SAM sites, and counter-air operations. For the electronic warfare part a number of Boeing 707s, fitted with a variety of electronic warfare equipment, flew well to the rear (out of range of the missiles) and their equipment automatically identified the missile site radars and then jammed them; communications systems, which are essential in any integrated air-defence system, were also jammed.

The second stage was to send over numbers of drones to simulate attacking Israeli aircraft. As these approached the Syrian air-defence networks the radars were activated to track them, and shortly afterwards the Syrian batteries started to launch missiles at the drones.

As soon as the Syrian SAMs started to engage the drones, Israeli air force Phantoms, armed with American-supplied AGM-78 Standard ARMs (anti-radiation missiles) and AGM-45 Shrike ARMs

attacked each battery. Before the missile is launched, the aircraft carrying the AGM-78, normally a Phantom, receives the hostile radar signal, which is then processed to determine the location and type of target; this information is then passed to the missile, which is then launched and homes onto the target. As soon as the radar of the Syrian SAM batteries were destroyed, waves of strike aircraft, including Skyhawks and Kfir-C2s, went in and attacked the missile sites with standard iron bombs and cluster-type weapons, the latter being of particular use against the batteries which, with their associated supporting equipment (generators, reloaders and command caravans), tend to be spread out. With these techniques 17 out of the 19 batteries are believed to have been destroyed. It is also probable that the RPVs were in the area of the SAM sites during the attacks to enable the Israeli commanders to the rear to monitor the effectiveness of the attacks closely and to confirm exactly which batteries had been destroyed and which were only damaged and therefore needed an additional strike.

To protect it, SAM suppression aircraft of the Israeli air force employed the Grumman E-2C Hawkeye AEW aircraft as an airborne command post with McDonnell Douglas F-15 and General Dynamics F-16 aircraft flying top cover. The E-2C could detect the Syrian MiG-21 and MiG-23 aircraft as they took off from their bases in Syria, and the Israelis were then able to position their aircraft before the Syrians arrived over Lebanon. Syrian fighters rely heavily on ground control to make a successful interception, and the Boeing 707s jammed the communications links between the fighter and ground stations to such effect that often the Syrian fighters had little idea where the Israeli aircraft were coming from until it was too late.

At a later date several of the more modern SA-8 'Gecko' batteries were successfully destroyed in the Lebanon, and in August and September the same year at least 10 SA-9 'Gaskin' batteries were also destroyed by the Israeli air force.

Israeli RPVs (remotely piloted vehicles) flew close to Syrian positions, enticing their radar controllers into action, drawing fire from SAM batteries. Once the opposing radars were activated Phantoms fired their AGM-78 anti-radiation missiles, which homed in on the Syrian radar transmissions and destroyed the equipment.

Without radar control, Syrian SA-6 batteries were helpless and unless moved away fast became sitting targets for Israeli strike aircraft following up.

1982: The Road to Beirut

An Israeli air force F-4E Phantom spirals over West Beirut as it releases a decoy flare to mislead any heat-seeking missiles being fired against it by PLO defence units in the city below.

This Israeli Centurion operating in the suburbs of Beirut, is well equipped for the close-range combat role by a 0.5-in (12.7-mm) heavy machine-gun at the front of the turret and two 0.3-in (7.62-mm) machine guns on the roof.

ceeded to use what artillery and mobile rocket-launchers they had to bombard the approaching Israeli forces. It was at this stage that the agony of Beirut began as the Israelis countered with massive artillery, mortar and rocket bombardments of their own. The inhabitants of Beirut suffered terribly during this period and the world watched as a city was seemingly destroyed. Internal public opinion was arrayed against the Israelis, who pounded the suspected PLO positions without mercy until the point was reached where the world rebelled at the sight of 175-mm (6.89-in) M107 self-propelled guns with a potential range of 32 miles (51 km) being used to knock out single sniper positions in apartment blocks at a range of only several hundred metres.

It was time to call a halt. World opinion rallied the United Nations and especially the United States into putting pressure on the Israelis to stop the killing. The PLO had by then had more than enough and was willing to leave, so under the terms of a cease-fire the PLO left Beirut and was (officially) scattered in small groups around the Arab world. (In fact many of them made their way back to Lebanon via Syria and were back again in action during the factional fighting of 1983.) The Israelis moved into Beirut and took over the massive PLO weapon and supply stockpiles that had

During the Lebanon campaign the Israeli navy gave support by shelling suspected Arab guerrilla positions near the coast (as seen here) or landing commando parties for raids on supply dumps or camps.

been accumulated.

Things seemed set for a peaceful return to Israel, but then things took their usual nasty turn. The massacres that took place in the remaining Palestinian refugee camps around Beirut were blamed upon the Israeli forces, although they were carried out by one or other of the various militias that swarmed around the city, and it was not long before feelings against the Israelis grew to such a pitch that they were being assaulted on all sides by 'resistance' and other groups determined to see them out of Lebanon. 'Peace for Galilee' had by then grown out of all proportion to its original aims, and after a period of political wrangling in Jerusalem the Israelis withdrew, their places being apparently taken by an internal peace-keeping force. What actually happened was that the various feuding factions once more set about each other and turned Beirut into as much a battleground as it had been the previous October.

The Israelis did not return all the way to Israel. Instead they took up positions along a line from the sea following the line of the Awali river. Here they constructed huge earth and concrete fortifications that (at the time of writing) seem set to form the new border of Israel with what is left of Lebanon.

Peace seems as far away as ever.

Far right: A Merkava tank in front of a Palestine Liberation Organization (PLO) headquarters near the centre of Beirut. The Merkava has its main engine at the front of the hull to give extra protection for the crew.

The Israeli Army

The Israeli army is the largest component of the Israeli armed forces, and usually has to bear the largest load during any military operation. It is unique in that all Israelis (men and women) have to fulfil a regular commitment to military service, whilst the core of regular soldiers is small. They are well provided with large amounts of good, modern weapons, and they have repeatedly proved themselves to be masters of modern armoured warfare. Their infantry units are as good as any in the world, and their artillery is superb. But they are still a citizen army that fights for survival; that fact provides them with an edge that makes them win.

Left: Upgraded Centurion tank of the Israeli Armoured Corps move up to the front. Of note are the infra-red driving light and spare track links to the glacis plate, and the commander's machine-gun.

Below: The latest tank to enter service is the Israeli-designed and built Merkava, which has the same M68 105-mm gun as fitted to the M60, M48A5 and Upgraded Centurion tanks.

The IDF/A has been brought to its present structure by entirely pragmatic means learned through experience in combat and the adoption of tactics that suit the weapons with which the force is armed.

One of the basic tenet to grasp regarding the IDF/A is that accepting Israeli nationality imposes drastic military requirements upon the individual. Every Israeli man or woman has to accept some form of military commitment, the only exceptions being made in extreme circumstances of health or religion. Every man or woman has initially to serve in the army, navy or air force for at least 39 months (24 months for women). After that period they then pass to the reserves and carry out an annual period of training or service with their unit until they reach the age of 54 (34 or marriage

for women) but by the time many reach that age they have already passed to the local home guard units or other type of local defence units. The usual home defence unit is the *Haganah Merchavit* or Home Defence Group. In some urban areas many of the older personnel move into civil defence units.

For the Israeli civilians who are to become soldiers, a rigorous pre-selection process is carried out. Those with seemingly the highest abilities and technical leanings are selected for the technical branches, usually the Armour Corps. Others are directed according to their abilities. Officers and NCOs are selected only after spending a period of time in the ranks, although some recruits from certain special schools and colleges where some military training is provided

The Israeli Army

become NCOs almost as soon as they join the service. After selection for commissioned rank, the recruits carry out a lengthy and intensive period of training that requires them to stay in the army for 30 months more than their normal period of full-time service. Some of their initial officer training includes a platoon commander's course based on that used by the *Palmach*.

The IDF/A has 16 corps. These are the Armour (including the armoured infantry); Artillery; Infantry and Parachute; Engineers; Signals; Ordnance; Supply and Transport; General Services; Women's; Medical; Military Police; Education; the Rabbinate; the Judge Advocate's Branch; Military Intelligence; and the *Nahal* (the 'Fighting Pioneer Youth' the modern equivalent of the old *Palmach* and formed from young people who form and defend *kibbutzim* in border or remote areas).

The actual number of men and women actually serving at any one time is a closely guarded secret, although estimates put the numbers in service at any one time at about 135,000. Of this number about 110,000 are conscripts, both men and women, with the rest acting as the regular leadership and training cadre. The full force could be raised to approximately 450,000 in an emergency if all the available reserves are recalled for service, but in the past this has happened only infrequently. At any one time a number of reservists are always in training with their units, and some IDF/A operations or responses to external threats can be met by recalling only a limited number from the reserves. The mobilization process can be described only as super-efficient. Every reservist has his or her code word that will require them to return to their unit. These code words are transmitted over the radio, flashed onto television screens and in some instances transmitted by telephone or telegram. Once the code word is received the reservist then grabs the uniform with which he has been issued to keep at home and makes his way as best he can to his unit's location (the same applies to the women soldiers, although they more often make for base areas while the men move to field locations). The journey is made by any means possible. Public transport is an obvious method (all bus and other transport depots are regarded as military locations and are guarded by the older reservists accordingly), but hitch-hiking has been raised to a level unheard-of in other countries and many reservists have found their way to their units in this fashion in past emergencies.

155-mm (6.1-in) self-propelled M-50 howitzer of the IDF/A about to be fired. The M-50 is a rebuilt Sherman tank chassis fitted with a French Model 50 155-mm howitzer at the rear of the hull.

Once at his unit, the reservist is issued with a personal weapon, ammunition and any other necessary kit. The whole process has often taken less than a day in the past and from civilian life to service in action can often take little over 24 hours, sometimes less. The degree of personal motivation of rejoin a unit in an emergency is high, and many stories have been recorded of reservists going to extreme lengths to reach their posts. The whole process is often rehearsed, but usually on a small scale, as a full-scale mobilization disrupts the economic and social life of the nation to a degree unacceptable to many nations and each exercise costs the national exchequer a sum that severely limits the number of times it can be carried out.

In action the highest Israeli operational formation is the brigade, but this title is something of a misnomer, the term 'battle group' perhaps being more appropriate. Each brigade may be variable in content, for the make-up and form of the units involved will vary to suit the brigade's operational task and the nature of the ground over which it is to operate. As an extreme example, a brigade operating in the desert regions will have a higher tank and other armoured content than a

An Israeli infantry patrol armed with 5.56-mm Galil assault rifles moves forward, covered by an M60A1 tank fitted with the Blazer active armour that provides protection against RPG-7s.

An old American half-track rebuilt by Israel, with a Detroit-Diesel engine and ball-mounted machine-gun to the right of the driver. These are still in service in large numbers.

brigade selected to operate in the mountains of the Golan. Thus only a rough guide can be provided.

As the armoured brigade is one of the most important and numerous in the IDF/A (there are 33 of them), it would be as well to examine one of them. At the top there is the Armoured Brigade Headquarters containing signals, intelligence and other such elements, including the necessary administration elements. Under this headquarters are three tank battalions, one mechanized infantry battalion normally equipped with M113 armoured personnel carriers (APCs), a reconnaissance company and a 120-mm (4.72-in) mortar battalion. Each of the three tank battalions has a headquarters nucleus of three main battle tanks (MBTs) with four tank companies under its command. In its turn each tank company has its own headquarters with two MBTs commanding three platoons each with three tanks. Thus in this typical tank battalion there are 47 MBTs, although some battalions have as few as 35 MBTs and some over 50 MBTs.

Each armoured brigade also has its own repair workshop with a recovery section or sections, a logistic unit and a signals unit over and above the brigade headquarters unit. Some brigades also have a combat engineer unit, but in every armoured brigade there are, down to company level, MBTs fitted with specialist engineer equipment such as dozer blades and mine-clearing ploughs or rollers.

Apart from the 33 known armoured brigades there are 10 mechanized infantry brigades, five of them trained for the paradrop role. There are also 12 territorial and border infantry brigades, some of which are *Nahal* militia. To support all these units there are 15 artillery brigades, each of which has five battalions. Each of the artillery battalions has three batteries.

This full force cannot be maintained at all times. The normal peacetime establishment may vary slightly, but is generally kept at five armoured brigades, four mechanized infantry brigades and two airborne/parachute brigades. These units are issued with the best equipment available, the other brigades being issued with whatever else is to hand. As will be mentioned below, this 'whatever else' may be drawn from a wide variety of types of equipment, but the smallest unit that is equipped with a single type of equipment is the battalion. Thus an armoured brigade could be equipped, theoretically, with three different types of MBT, but each of those three types would be distributed as one type to a battalion.

To suit the operational requirements on local fronts it is possible that brigades will be organized into a division. This has happened in the past and at such times the division has been named after its commander (this use of commander's names to identify formations is sometimes used at lower levels). An armoured division could consist of three armoured brigades, one artillery brigade, a reconnaissance battalion (equipped with both MBTs and APCs), an engineer battalion, signals and logistics units and other supporting units such as mobile workshops. On paper the IDF/A can muster 11 such armoured divisions, but it is doubtful if anything like that number would ever be fielded.

Equipment

The IDF/A has in the past nearly always been chronically short of weapons. This was especially true in the early days of the *Haganah* and the desperate years of the struggle for independence. Since then the Israelis have been forced to obtain weapons and other equipment from whatever sources they can find. In the years immediately following independence this was France and, surprisingly enough, Czechoslovakia. At

one time the United Kingdom supplied large amounts of equipment, including Centurion MBTs, but in recent years the mantle of equipment supplier has passed to the United States, which is now politically and financially committed to maintaining weapon and equipment supplies.

But Israel has in the past learned not to rely on outside sources for military assistance: arms deliveries from overseas can be held up or terminated to suit short-term political or economic policies following some course of action that the Israeli government has felt necessary to carry out. Nor can Israel rely on her enemies as a source of supply although past campaigns have often resulted in vast quantities of war booty,

An IDF/A tank column advances across the desert with 105-mm (4.13-in) guns pointing in each direction, ready to respond to any sudden attack from any quarter.

The M548 tracked cargo carrier, a member of the M113 family of tracked vehicles, is used by the IDF/A to support 155-mm and 175-mm artillery batteries.

industry, manufacturing everything from uniforms to MBTs and ammunition. This industry operates under the overall title of Israel Military Industries or IMI, although a large number of concerns is involved under the IMI banner. The success of this industrial venture is such that IMI now operate a thriving export armaments business in many parts of the world, including the United States, bringing in much needed foreign revenue to offset some of the Israeli defence budget costs. Into this category come the Uzi sub-machine gun, the Galil assault rifle and various mine-clearing devices fitted to MBTs, some of which now grace the front of the American M1 Abrams MBT.

IMI also makes nearly all its own ammunition, both small arms and artillery, including tank gun ammunition. Again, much of this is exported and the armour-piercing projectile developed by IMI is now used by the MBTs of several NATO armies.

Despite all this internal design, development and manufacture, Israel still depends to a large extent on outside supplies. The facilities for manufacture within Israel are relatively limited, and the nation has few raw material resources, so even though Israel now has its own indigenous MBT design in the Merkava it still finds it necessary to purchase numbers of American M60 MBTs and numerous other types of armoured vehicle. It also has to depend on outside sources for much of the funding required to obtain weapons. In the past this has led to reliance on the international Jewish community, but of late the Americans have increasingly offered either long-term loans or other relatively cheap forms of funding.

The end result of all this procurement of weapons and equipment is that the IDF/A is now equipped with a very varied range of equipment from many parts of

A graveyard of Soviet supplied tanks captured by Israel during conflicts in the Middle East. Some of these were subsequently modified and used by the IDF/A.

A T-54 in service with the IDF/A after the 1973 Middle East conflict. This particular tank retains its original 100-mm gun.

much of which has been taken into Israeli service, often after a programme of modernization to suit the equipment to Israeli requirements. Into this latter category come the many ex-Soviet T-54/T-55 MBTs that have been captured in past wars; they are now equipped with 105-mm (4.13-in) guns, new electrics and electronics.

To reduce the possibility of interruptions the Israelis have now established their own indigenous arms

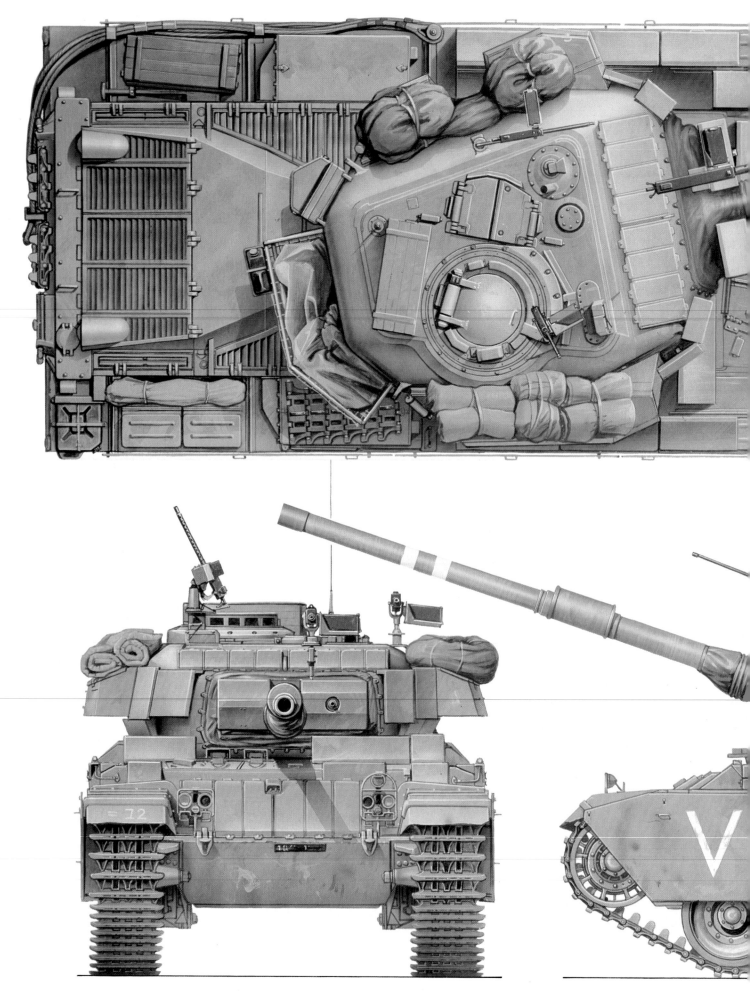

Upgraded Centurion Main Battle Tank

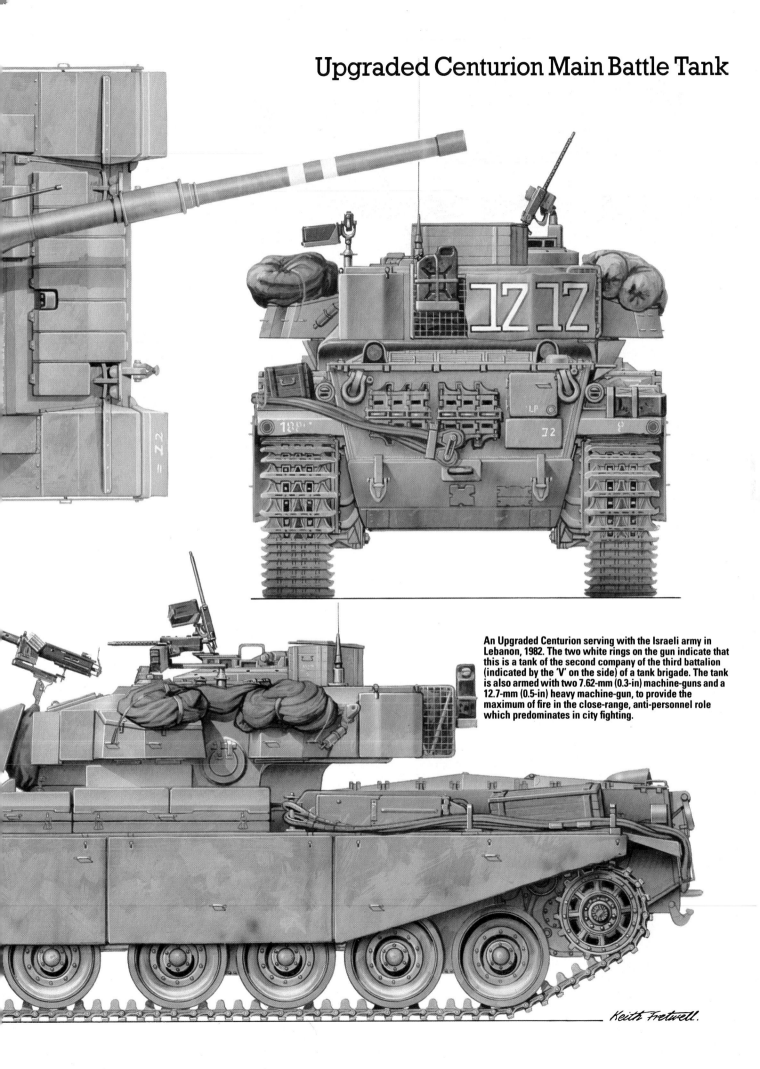

An Upgraded Centurion serving with the Israeli army in Lebanon, 1982. The two white rings on the gun indicate that this is a tank of the second company of the third battalion (indicated by the 'V' on the side) of a tank brigade. The tank is also armed with two 7.62-mm (0.3-in) machine-guns and a 12.7-mm (0.5-in) heavy machine-gun, to provide the maximum of fire in the close-range, anti-personnel role which predominates in city fighting.

Keith Fretwell.

The Israeli Army

the world. To keep it all in operating order and to supply all the necessary spare parts must be a quartermaster's nightmare, a nightmare that is not made any simpler by the fact that virtually no item is ever discarded. When replaced by something better or more modern, each item is passed to the reserves, or placed into storage or given to the various home-defence units. Thus it is not impossible to see an elderly home guard member guarding a bus station with an old World War II 7.92-mm Mauser rifle slung over his shoulder. Despite the fact that the Israeli 'tankies' have learned to dislike the little French AMX-13 light tanks, some are still to be found on the strength of reconnaissance companies in some armoured brigades. Numerous other examples of this tendency could be quoted, but they are perhaps better left to the sections dealing with the various arms of the service.

The Armour Corps

It has been estimated that the IDF/A has a strength of no fewer than 3,600 MBTs. In the context of a manpower strength of 450,00 this is a remarkable total, and is far greater a ratio of armour to soldiers than in many other armies, if not actually the greatest. The cream of the available conscripts and the best of the officers go to the Armour Corps. It is not unusual to find in the Armour Corps officers who are far younger for their rank than any other army (colonels/brigade commanders at 35 are not uncommon) and they have at their disposal some very sophisticated equipment.

The strength of the Armour Corps rests with two basic types of MBT, the Centurion and the American M60. Although accurate figures are not likely to become available, it has been estimated that the Israelis have approximately 1,100 Centurions and 1,010 M60s, with another 125 M60s to be delivered from the United States. Of the two types the Centurion has been in service the longer.

When the first Centurions were issued to the Armour Corps in 1959 they were far more complex vehicles than any tank previously operated by the IDF/A. Up until then the main strength of the Armour Corps was invested in elderly Shermans, and the Centurion was a great deal more complicated to use and maintain than the World War II stalwart. Despite these early problems the crews soon learned to appreciate the powerful main gun and the excellent armour of the Centurion, although the Meteor petrol engines gave constant trouble in the Israeli environment. In the late 1960s it was decided to upgrade the in-service Centurions by

A T-55 of the IDF/A with its original 100-mm gun replaced by the standard American designed 105-mm M68, which is in fact a British L7 made under licence.

M60A1 Main Battle Tank

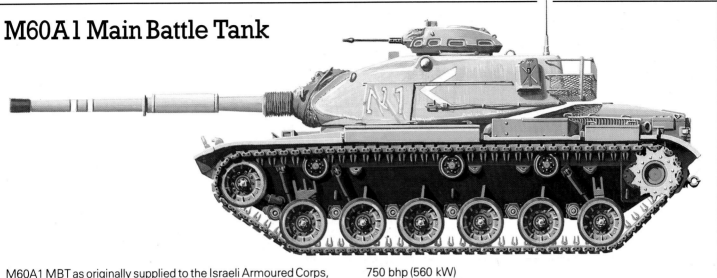

M60A1 MBT as originally supplied to the Israeli Armoured Corps, fitted with a commander's cupola armed with a 0.5-in (12.7-mm) machine-gun. These have since been removed and a new low-profile cupola installed.

Specification

Crew: 4

Weight: 48.98 tonnes

Engine: Continental AVDS-1790-2A 12-cylinder diesel developing 750 bhp (560 kW)

Dimensions: length (with gun forward) 30 ft 11½ in (9.44 m); length (hull) 22 ft 9½ in (6.95 m); width 11 ft 11 in (3.63 m); height 10 ft 8¼ in (3.27 m)

Performance: maximum road speed 30 mph (48.28 km/h); maximum road range 310 miles (500 km); fording 4 ft 0 in (1.22 m); gradient 60%; vertical obstacle 3 ft 0 in (0.91 m); trench 8 ft 6 in (2.59 m)

Israel's Centurion force has proved itself the master of many more recently designed tanks. Re-engined and with the superb British-designed 105-mm gun, the Centurion will remain a potent force on the battlefield for many years to come.

fitting a new diesel engine. At the same time the opportunity was taken to ensure that all vehicles were fitted with the 105-mm (4.13-in) main gun, a new electrical system was installed, a new braking system was fitted, the ammunition stowage in the turret was revised to allow more rounds to be carried, and more fuel capacity was added. The result was an MBT that resembled a Centurion but differed from it in significant ways, and the resultant vehicle is now the mainstay of the Armour Corps. Numerous other modifications have been added over the years. Israeli tank crews always seem to accumulate extra kit and consequently extra external stowage has been added to the turret bustle of many Centurions. It is also possible to fit a set of several types of locally-manufactured engineer equipments to the Centurion as well as to nearly every other type of MBT in service with the Armour Corps. Included in this range of equipment is a dozer blade for clearing battlefield obstacles, mine rollers and mine ploughs. The list of other special extras is quite long but many of these extras can be used by other Armour Corps MBTs.

Typical of these extras is the Clear Lane Marking System, or CLAMS, a metal box fitted to the rear of a Centurion fitted with mine-clearing equipment. As the Centurion clears its way through the minefield it drops small self-illuminating posts onto the ground to define the cleared lane for following infantry and other MBTs. Infra-red driving lights for night use are another extra, but one of the most unusual pieces of extra equipment was first identified during the 1982 advance into Lebanon. For some years past it had been noticed that most Israeli MBTs, including Centurions, were liberally provided with small metal hooks all over their armoured exteriors. The purpose of these hooks gave rise to much speculation as to their function, the main channel of thought being that they supported some form of extra armour to improve protection. The Lebanon advances revealed the truth to the curious observers, for the hooks proved to be supporting an array of small plates that added protection to the carrier tank but not in the way first supposed. The plates were in fact a type of protection known as active armour. Active armour is a form of defence against the hollow-charge projectile fired by many types of anti-tank weapon from the rocket projector to the gun: when the hollow charge hits an armoured target the warhead forms a long jet of intensely hot flame that burns its way through the armour plate to destroy the vehicle interior and the crew. The active armour prevents this from happening, for at the instant the jet is formed the active armour detonates to disrupt or deflect the jet away from the armour underneath it. The Israelis are probably the first to employ this type of protection on their MBTs, and they have now reached the stage where it is being offered for export sales under the IMI designation Blazer. IMI claim that the weight of Blazer plates to protect an MBT would weigh no more than 4,409 lb (2000 kg), and that sets of plates to cover almost any MBT design could be produced.

Blazer has also been fitted to the numerous M60s in service with the Armour Corps. Like the Centurion the M60 is fitted with the 105-mm (4.13-in) main gun and has a diesel engine. The M60 can carry and use all the various extras that are carried by the Centurion. Most of the M60s are of the M60A1 configuration, but the more recent additions have been the M60A3 with an improved fire-control system and other modifications. These two types are not mixed within the battalion, to

The Israeli Army

ease the logistic and repair loads. A tank battalion has either the M60A1 or the M60A3, and the variant now on order is the M60A3.

Both the Centurion and the M60 are powerful fighting vehicles well capable of standing up to anything Israel's hostile neighbours are likely to be able to put into the field in the foreseeable future. Even the advent of the Soviet T-62 and the more recent T-72 in Syrian hands has not diminished the Israeli armour's dominance on the Middle East battlefields, for during the Lebanon operations the Israelis proved to be well able to tackle the T-62 with its 105-mm (4.13-in) gun, and even the T-72 with its 125-mm (4.92-in) main gun came off worse in several encounters. Included in these encounters was another 105-mm (4.13-in) gun-armed tank, and one that has attracted a great deal of attention around the world: the Israeli Merkava (chariot).

The Merkava was designed, developed and manufactured in Israel itself, entirely to IDF/A specifications and intended for operations in the particular tank warfare conditions of Middle East battlefields. It was produced from the operational analysis of the results of the 1967 war, when Israeli tank commanders decided that modern armoured warfare protection mattered more than mobility, a philosophy unfavoured by many European experts. As they had considerably more combat experience than the experts, the Israelis went ahead with the design and development of a new design of tank, and by 1977 the first examples were ready for inspection. The new design was called Merkava and revealed many innovations.

For a start the Merkava has the main engine at the front instead of the more orthodox rear. In simple terms this means that the engine will provide more frontal protection for the crew, which numbers four. At the rear of the hull there are two large doors which can be used for two purposes. One is the rapid replenishment of ammunition, and the other the rapid escape of the crew in an emergency such as a fatal hit. Yet another possibility is that the space inside the doors can be used to carry a small number of infantrymen or combat

M60A1s of the Israeli Armour Corps at a depot in Israel. Of interest is the covered-up two 7.62-mm (0.31-in) machine-guns on the turret roof and 12.7-mm (0.5-in) machine-gun over the 105-mm (4.13-in) gun, and attachment points for Blazer active armour.

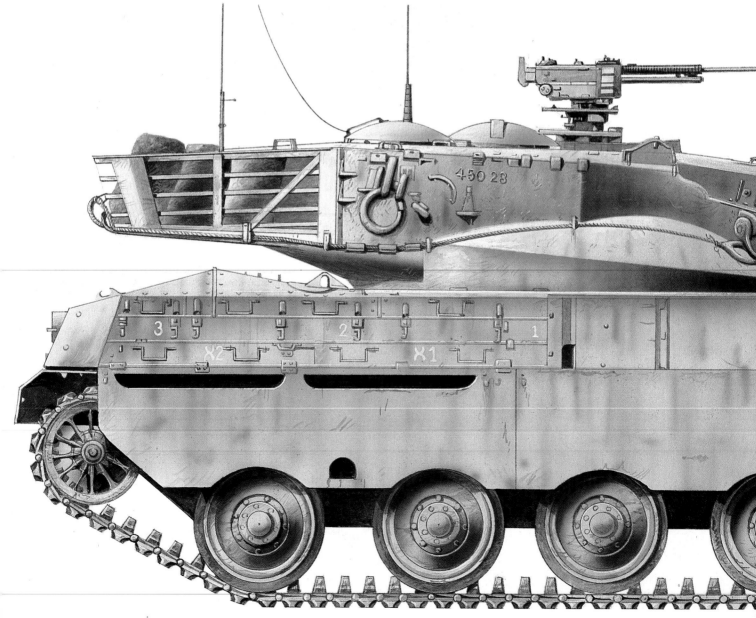

Above: An Upgraded Centurion tank moves forwards towards the front. Today the Israeli army is the largest user of the Centurion, with over 1,000 in front-line service.

The Merkava has an unusual configuration with the engine and driver at the front, turret in the centre and additional ammunition being carried at the rear of the hull. By 1984 nearly 300 had been built.

engineers into action, where they can dismount for any number of special purposes. The Merkava also has a wedge-shaped turret that combines good armour protection with the ability to deflect solid shot away from the target. Side skirts protect the hull and suspension against close-range hollow-charge missiles, and even the driver's hatch and the turret machine-gun embrasure are provided with carefully-stepped armour to provide extra protection by deflecting small-arms fire away from the vulnerable vision or firing slits. For fire-control the Merkava has an Israeli digital computer-controlled system allied to a laser range-finder, and various sensors to assess the various external factors that can affect the gun's external ballistics are scattered around the top of the turret. For all its protection the Merkava still has a useful road speed of 27.3 mph (44 km/h) compared with the Centurion's 21.75 mph (35 km/h), due mainly to the 900-hp (671-kW) diesel engine fitted.

Already the Merkava Mk 3 is under development for introduction into service by about 1985. The Merkava Mk 3 will have even more crew protection, and this alone is a measure of the importance that the IDF/A places upon the survival of its tank crews in action. A great deal of money, time and effort is expended by the IDF/A in training tank crews (especially the officers), and in many ways they are regarded as the cream of the Army. Consequently the Merkava has been produced mainly to provide them with increased protec-

tion and the resultant design is one that has aroused interest from abroad. To date just over 200 Merkavas have been produced and are in service with the IDF/A. Already the Merkava Mk 2 is in being, but it is understood that this will be passed over in favour of the Merkava Mk 3 on the production lines and that only a relatively small batch of Merkava Mk 2s will therefore be built.

So the Merkava has joined the Centurion and the M60 in the armoured brigades, but is not the only other MBT in service with the IDF/A. There are also in service some 650 M48s, all of which have now been locally modified to M48A5 standard with a 105-mm (4.13-in) main gun, a diesel engine and a new low-profiled commander's cupola. The M48s originally came from West Germany during the late 1960s until Arab pressure caused that source of supply to cease. Not long afterwards the United States assumed the supply of M48s and the type is now an important item in the armoured brigade tank parks. The M48 was a forerunner of the M60, differing from the later MBT only in detail now that the modification update has been completed. Incidentally, the new low profile commander's cupola has been such a success in service that it has now been retrofitted to US Army M48s.

Mention must also be made of the large number of ex-Soviet MBTs in Israeli service. The bulk of these number about 440, and are a mix of virtually identical T-54s and T-55s. These were captured in the Six-Day

This Merkava Mk 1 MBT has attachment points mounted under the nose of its hull for roller-type mine clearing equipment. Israel captured such equipment from the Arabs and subsequently designed a much improved version.

M48A3 Main Battle Tank

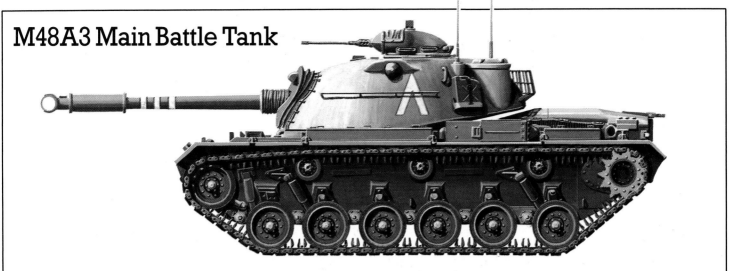

M48A3 of the Israeli Armoured Corps as used in the 1967 conflict. After this most Israeli M48s were fitted with a diesel engine, 105-mm (4.13-in) gun and other modifications to bring them up to M48A5 standard as used by the US Army.

Specification
Crew: 4
Weight: 47.17 tonnes
Engine: Continental AVDS-1790-2A 12-cylinder diesel developing

750 bhp (560 kW)
Dimensions: length (with gun forward) 28 ft 6 in (8.69 m); length (hull) 22 ft 7 in (6.88 m); width 11 ft 11 in (3.63 m); height 10 ft 3 in (3.12 m)
Performance: maximum road speed 40 mph (48.2 km/h); maximum range 288 miles (463 km); fording 4 ft 0 in (1.22 m); gradient 60%; vertical obstacle 3 ft 0 in (0.92 m); trench 8 ft 6 in (2.59 m)

and later Yom Kippur Wars, and a few more have been obtained during the various border raids carried out before the major invasion of Lebanon in 1982 (which produced yet more booty). About 250 of the T-54s and T-55s are now held in reserve against some future requirement, and are not usually used in action as their presence on any battlefield could cause understandable problems of identification. These reserve tanks have been fitted with the usual 105-mm (4.13-in) gun, a 12.7-mm (0.5-in) machine-gun in place of the ex-Soviet equivalent, a new electrical system and a new fire-control system. In this form the ex-Soviet tanks are known by the designation TI-67.

Israel also has in reserve about 150 captured Soviet T-62s armed with a 115-mm (4.53-in) gun. No alterations have apparently been made to these MBTs, and

they too are apparently held in reserve against some future contingency. It may well be that these tanks form the equipment of a few tank battalions of the reserves.

As mentioned above, some of the older equipment still survives. The most numerous examples of these include the Sherman tanks that formed part of the equipment of the newly-emergent Armour Corps in the 1950s. Over the years the Shermans, many of which were taken into the Israeli fold from surplus sales and scrap yards all over the world, have been gradually up-gunned, fitted with increased armour and generally modernized. But even with all these extras the Shermans are now obsolete and lack the general protection that more modern tanks provide, and they have now almost all been phased out of front-line service. Most of the few that were left in 1982 were handed over

The crew of an Israeli L-33 155-mm (6.1-in) self-propelled howitzer man their vehicle. This system, designed and converted in Israel, was first used in the 1973 conflict against Syria and Egypt.

A Trail Blazer engineer vehicle, based on the chassis of the M74 armoured recovery vehicle and fitted with a hydraulic dozer blade, crane, stabilizing blade at hull rear and winches.

to the various Christian militias who held fief in southern Lebanon before and during the invasion of that country. There many still remain as they are well able to tackle any type of armoured vehicle that the PLO and other opposing militias are likely to be able to field. By the time the Israelis had finished with them, the Shermans had little in common with the World War II original. Many of them had been fitted with ex-French 105-mm (4.13-in) guns and even the relatively unimproved Shermans had long 75-mm (2.95-in) guns. Most of the Shermans still in use with the IDF/A have now been converted into special-purpose vehicles which will be discussed below.

As mentioned earlier, a few French AMX-13 light tanks still remain in some units, and are now mainly used for the reconnaissance role. For a while during the 1960s the Israelis used them as light tanks for the simple reason that they had nothing else, but the little tanks proved to be unsuitable for the stand-up-fight role the Israelis required as they lacked protection, and the oscillating turret proved to be a source of trouble and a potential hazard in battle. The few left are now due to be phased out of service: their turrets will no doubt be used for some form of local defence of outlying *kibbutzim* and other locations. This local-defence use of old tank turrets (usually fixed in concrete but retaining 360° traverse) is not a new idea, but one that the Israelis have adopted to bolster some of their border and other local-defence schemes. Most of these static turrets are very difficult to spot as they are extensively camouflaged for extra protection and to enhance the surprise effect against any approaching enemy. The hulls that remain once the turrets have been removed are used either for driver training or for conversion into special-purpose vehicles (AMX-13 chassis have been used to carry LAR 160 artillery rocket launchers). Some are also used as tractors for both military and civil purposes.

M51 Sherman tank with turret traversed to the rear. This tank is armed with the French 105-mm (4.13-in) D1504 gun, which is basically a shortened version of the 105-mm CH-105-F1 installed in the AMX-30 MBT.

In addition to being fitted with a 105-mm (4.13-in) gun, the M51 Sherman has been rebuilt and fitted with a Cummins diesel engine developing 460 hp (343 kW). During the 1973 Middle East war it successfully engaged T-62 MBTs.

the armoured brigades, or towed, as with nearly all the other brigades. The self-propelled artillery has to keep up with the tanks as they move, and as some of the mechanized infantry formations have to keep their artillery with them as they dash in all directions, some of these units also use self-propelled artillery.

With such a wide and varied range of ordnance to mention it would be as well to start at the top and work downwards, although this does not reflect the hierarchy of calibres involved. In theory the larger calibres are usually kept under high-level control, but in practice heavy calibres may well come under the control of brigade commanders. As has been mentioned above, the Israeli brigade is very much an ad hoc battle grouping of units to suit a defined operational task, and if heavy artillery is required it will be included.

Top in the striking power available to the IDF/A are their atomic weapons. The Israelis have long denied that they have such weapons, but it is now an open secret that atomic weapons do exist in the Israeli armoury. They are no doubt being held against some dire emergency that would threaten the state. Although the IDF/AF would clearly be the main user of such weapons, the IDF/A has the capability to fire such nuclear warheads with their American Lance surface-to-surface artillery missiles, which have a range of up to 75 miles (120 km). The Lance is used as a potential nuclear-warhead carrier by several NATO nations, and it would be surprising if the Israelis did not do the same, for the Lance is an expensive weapon system demanding in manpower and resources. The Lance is carried into action on a tracked chassis which has been derived from that of the M113 armoured personnel carrier (also in Israeli service). Another tracked vehicle is used to carry a spare missile and some other equipment, but once in the firing position the Lance missile is elevated on the carrier and launched from a ramp on the vehicle. All the ballistic information required for the launch is fed into the missile's electronics before launch, and once launched the missile cannot be diverted from its intended path. The weight of a Lance at launch may be up to 3,375 lb (1530 kg), and the warhead itself weighs 465 lb (211 kg).

The Artillery

The attitude of the IDF/A towards the artillery is somewhat ambivalent. On one side it acknowledges that it cannot win wars without the use of artillery at all stages of a battle, yet at the same time it tends to regard the artillery as a dumping ground for the conscripts that cannot meet the requirements of the other arms. To counter this strange ambivalence the Artillery Corps conducts itself with a fierce professionalism and a determination to succeed.

The IDF/A has 15 artillery brigades, each of which has five battalions. Each battalion has its own headquarters element to command three batteries. Each battery has two or three troops under the command of its own small headquarters, and the normal number of guns to a troop is four. The main problem for the Artillery Corps is that its equipment is amongst the most widely varied in the IDF/A, and ranges from mortars to ballistic rockets. Thus a considerable portion of the IDF/A's logistic back-up is devoted towards supplying the artillery with ammunition and other such supplies. The problem is made no easier by the fact that the artillery may be either self-propelled, as with

A Lance surface-to-surface missile ready to launch from its tracked chassis, based on the M548 tracked cargo carrier. As far as is known, Israel only has conventional warheads for Lance, but the missile has nuclear capability.

Also on the rocket side of artillery, the Israelis are now large-scale operators of the multiple rocket-launchers that are generally known by their Russian name Katyusha. The Israelis have adopted this type of weapon after being on the receiving end of such weapons on many occasions, when the Soviets provided the Arabs and PLO guerrillas with Katyushas for use against Israeli targets. The Israelis noted the devastating effects on themselves and duly adopted the weapon. At first their equipments consisted solely of captured examples, but it was not long before they were manufacturing their own direct copies of the launchers and rockets. Today the Israelis are designing and producing their own versions so successfully that these are being sold to many other nations. Even so, many ex-Soviet equipments remain in large-scale service.

Rocket systems

Largest of the home-developed Israeli rockets is a 290-mm (11.42-in) multiple-launch rocket system about which little is known. In its development stages it provided an example of an old Sherman tank chassis being used for a specialized purpose, four of these large-calibre rockets being supported in a frame launcher.

Next down the rocket calibre scale is the 240-mm (9.45-in) multiple-launch rocket system. This is a direct copy of the Soviet BM-24 equipment. Thus it is possible to find both ex-Soviet and locally-produced 240-mm (9.45-mm) rocket systems in service. The Israeli system uses a 12-rocket launcher carried on the back of a 6×6 truck, and the rockets are fired ballistically with the objective of saturating the target area with explosive. The 240-mm (9.45-in) rocket is a powerful weapon. Weighing 244 lb (110.5 kg) at launch, each rocket has a warhead weighing 106.5 lb (48.3 kg) which detonates to produce a widespread splinter effect to enhance its lethality. Range is 11,700 yards (10700 m).

Further down the rocket calibre scale is a completely new Israeli system known as the LAR 160. The term has been derived from Light Artillery Rocket, 160 mm, for 160 mm (6.3 in) is the rocket calibre. The LAR 160 is designed as a far-reaching artillery rocket with a range of up to 32,800 yards (30000 m), and it has been designed in a modular form to be carried by several types of vehicle, both tracked and wheeled. The modular form comes from the fact that the rockets are pre-packed into sealed containers that double both as transport containers and launched tubes. These containers are loaded onto the launch vehicle and the rockets are fired from them without any further preparation. Once the rockets have been fired the container is discarded. Each rocket is 10 ft 10.33 in (3.311 m) long and weighs 243 lb (110 kg) at launch. The modular approach to the design is such that the rocket can carry 155-mm (6.1-in) conventional artillery warheads, or may alternatively be packed with bomblets or chemical payloads. The LAR 160 is already in service with the IDF/A and has been noted on old AMX-13 light tank and M48 tank hulls. The M809 6×6 truck has also been mentioned as a carrier and the M548 tracked cargo carrier has been discussed as another possible carrier, to the point where active approaches have been made to the US Army to adopt the LAR 160 in this form. Some exports have already been made (Venezuela is known to be one customer).

The only other multiple-launch artillery rocket system known to be in service with the IDF/A is the

Below: Israel captured such a large number of Soviet BM-24 (12-round) 240-mm (9.45-in) multiple rocket systems in the 1973 Middle East conflict that these were taken into service with the IDF/A. The rockets are now produced by Israel Military Industries.

Walid (4×4) armoured personnel carriers have been designed and built in Egypt and are fitted with a locally-produced 12-round multiple rocket system.

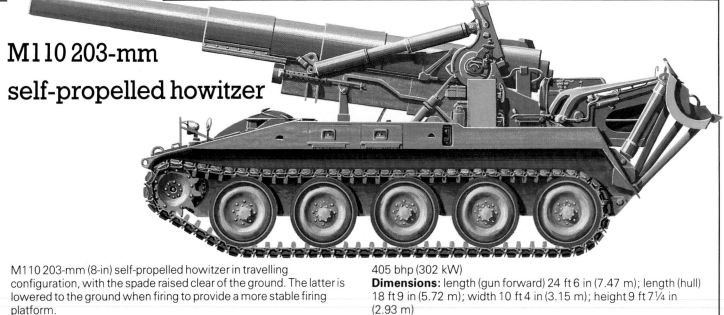

M110 203-mm self-propelled howitzer

M110 203-mm (8-in) self-propelled howitzer in travelling configuration, with the spade raised clear of the ground. The latter is lowered to the ground when firing to provide a more stable firing platform.

Specification
Crew: 5+8
Weight: 26.536 tonnes
Engine: one Detroit Diesel Model 8V-71T diesel developing 405 bhp (302 kW)

Dimensions: length (gun forward) 24 ft 6 in (7.47 m); length (hull) 18 ft 9 in (5.72 m); width 10 ft 4 in (3.15 m); height 9 ft 7¼ in (2.93 m)

Performance: maximum road speed 35 mph (56 km/h); maximum range 450 miles (725 km); gradient 60%; vertical obstacle 3 ft 4 in (1.016 m); trench 7 ft 9 in (2.362 m)

Soviet BM-21 122-mm (4.8-in) system. Large numbers of these have been captured in the past and many are now issued to some reserve artillery units. The BM-21 is carried on ex-Soviet 6×6 trucks, each truck carrying 40 rockets ready to fire. The range is over 21,875 yards (20000 m), and each rocket weighs either 170 lb (77 kg) or 101 lb (45.8 kg) depending on the type in use. Both rockets carry a warhead weighing 42.75 lb (19.4 kg).

Some other rocket types may be in use, for it is known that large numbers of ex-Soviet 122-mm (4.8-in) rockets on single-rocket launching ramps have been captured during anti-PLO raids, and it would be surprising if these were not used in some capacity by the Israelis.

M110 self-propelled howitzer

Moving to the conventional artillery side, the largest weapon used by the Artillery Corps is the American 8-in (203-mm) M110 self-propelled howitzer. According to some reports the IDF/A has 48 of these powerful howitzers, which also have a nuclear warhead poten-

tial, but it is not known if the Israelis use such warheads. In its original form the M110 has a range of 18,375 yards (16800 m) when firing a projectile weighing 204 lb (92.53 kg), but in recent years the Americans have fitted a new and longer barrel to the M110 which increases the possible range to 23,300 yards (21300 m). It is not certain at the time of writing whether or not the Israelis have taken up this option, but it would be surprising if they had not.

Next down the calibre line is the 175-mm (6.89-in) M107 self-propelled gun. This gun is carried on the same chassis as the M110, and the two weapons are interchangeable on the same chassis. The M107 is now being phased out of service with many other nations in favour of the long-range artillery rocket, but not so in Israel, for not only has the IDF/A some 140 already in service, it has even ordered more from the United States. The reason for this attraction to the M107 is simple: the range of the weapon suits the IDF/A well.

M110A2 203-mm self-propelled howitzer

The M110A2 203-mm (8-in) self-propelled howitzer is essentially the older M110 fitted with a longer barrel with a double baffle muzzle brake that enables it to fire ammunition with a higher muzzle velocity and longer range.

Specification
Crew: 5+8
Weight: 28.35 tonnes
Engine: one Detroit Diesel Model 8V-71T developing 405 bhp (302 kW)
Dimensions: length (gun forward) 36 ft 10½ in (10.73 m); length (hull) 18 ft 9 in (5.72 m); width 10 ft 4 in (3.15 m); height 10 ft 4 in (3.14 m)
Performance: maximum road speed 34 mph (54.7 km/h); maximum range 325 miles (523 km); gradient 60%; vertical obstacle 3 ft 4 in (1.016 m); trench 6 ft 3 in (1.91 m)

Left: A battery of IDF/A 175-mm (6.89-in) M107 self-propelled guns knocked out in the 1973 conflict. The slow rate of fire of these weapons makes them vulnerable to counter-battery fire and air attack.

Above: An M110 203-mm (8-in) self-propelled howitzer with a yellow identification panel on the glacis plate moves up towards the front line. Most of these howitzers are now being upgraded to the M110A2 standard.

The M107 gun barrel has a range of 35,750 yards (32,700 m), and it can fire a projectile weighing 147 lb (66.78 kg). This gun and projectile combination is ideal for the Israelis to fire into enemy rear areas, and it forms a perfect counter-bombardment weapon for use against the long-range artillery used by many Arab armies, in particular the ex-Soviet 180-mm (7.09-in) S-23 gun, which has a range of over 33,250 yards (30400 m) with conventional projectiles and even more with enhanced ammunition. The M107 can be recognized easily by its very long barrel, and is often seen in photographs of the IDF/A in action.

The next calibre down the scale is 155 mm (6.1 in), and here the Israelis have several types of equipment in service. The Israelis were the first to show the poten-

tial of the 155-mm (6.1-in) calibre in armoured warfare, their experience during the 1967 and 1973 wars demonstrating that 155 mm (6.1 in) was the smallest calibre that could effectively break up armoured attacks while they were still in the forming-up stage. Lighter calibres proved useless in this role, so 155 mm (6.1 in) has now become the accepted norm for all field artillery. The usual 155-mm (6.1-in) projectile is fired from howitzers and weighs about 95 lb (43 kg).

On the self-propelled artillery side the most important weapon is the American M109 and its longer variants, the M109A1 or M109A2. The basic M109 has a range of 15,975 yards (14600 m), while the longer-barrelled M109A1 or M109A2 can reach 19,800 yards (18100 m). Enhanced ammunition (using a rocket-

An M107 175-mm (6.89-in) self-propelled gun of the IDF/A in the firing position, with its hydraulically-operated spade lowered to the ground at the rear of the hull. Behind the M107 is the M548 tracked cargo carrier for ammunition.

An M110 203-mm (8-in) self-propelled howitzer of the IDF/A moves forward across the desert. The crew seated at the rear have no protection from small arms fire and shell splinters.

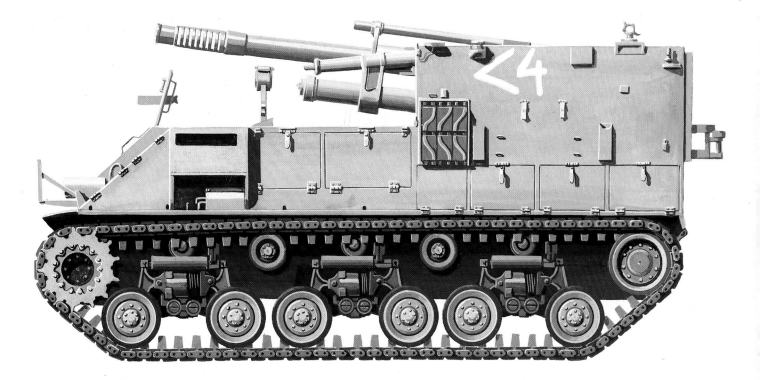

Above: Slowly being replaced in front-line service by the M109, the M-50 155-mm (6.1-in) self-propelled howitzer mounts what was originally a French-built towed howitzer on to what is basically a Sherman chassis. As the equipment withdraws from service, the chassis are converted into armoured ambulances or armoured artillery observation vehicles.

Right: An M109A1 self-propelled howitzer in its protective bunker somewhere on the Golan heights. In any future conflict, self-propelled artillery such as this would have to move around the battlefield in order to survive.

An M109A1 with 155-mm (6.1-in) ordnance in travel lock on the front of the hull. Of interest are the external stowage racks on the turret sides, which allows more space inside the turret for the crew to operate the weapon.

assisted projectile) can increase this range to 26,250 yards (24000 m), but at such ranges accuracy tends to deteriorate. The M109 carries its crew of six in an armoured turret and can even 'swim' across river obstacles, despite its weight of 52,470 lb (23800 kg). The Israelis have at least 300 M109s already in service and well over 100 are currently on order. They form the main artillery component of the armoured brigade artillery battalions.

Also still in service are about 300 155-mm (6.1-in) howitzers carried on converted Sherman chassis. There are two types of these, one being the L-33 and the other the M-50. The L-33 carries a 155-mm (6.1-in) Soltam howitzer in a large armoured box, and has been in service since 1973. It has a maximum range of 22,965 yards (21000 m). In contrast the M-50 has the howitzer in a relatively open armoured compartment and the howitzer is an ex-French Model 50 howitzer that was

M109A1 self-propelled howitzer

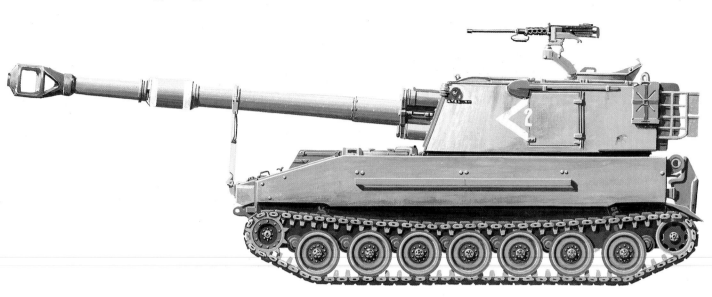

American-supplied M109A1 of the IDF/A, with the turret traversed forward and a 0.5-in (12.7-mm) M2 HB machine-gun mounted on the turret roof for anti-aircraft defence. The M109A1 is designated M109AL in Israeli service.

Specification
Crew: 6
Weight: 52,440 lb (23786 kg)
Engine: one Detroit Diesel Model 8V071T eight-cylinder diesel

developing 450 bhp (302 kW)
Dimensions: length (gun forward) 21 ft 8¼ in (6.612 m); length (hull) 20 ft 6¼ in (6.26 m); width 10 ft 9¾ in (3.30 m); height 10 ft 9½ in (3.29 m)
Performance: maximum road speed 35 mph (56 km/h); maximum range 240 miles (390 km); gradient 60%; vertical obstacle 1 ft 9 in (0.53 m); trench 6 ft 0 in (1.828 m)

---

sold to Israel as a towed weapon but which has now been converted to the self-propelled role. The maximum range of this howitzer is 19,250 yards (17600 m). The L-33 and the M-50 will remain in use for some time to come but they are now being gradually phased out of use with front-line brigades as more modern equipment (usually the M109A1) comes into service.

On the towed side, the largest towed weapons in service are 155-mm (6.1-in) howitzers. There are two main types, with another coming into service in the near future. They are both Soltam howitzers, the M-71 and the M-68 with almost identical performances: for instance, both weapons have a maximum range of 25,700 yards (23500 m). Both have large split-trail field carriages and both are heavy. It is this latter point that has led to the introduction of a further version, the M-81, which has an auxiliary power unit attached to one of the trail legs to provide power to move the gun over short distances, to provide the power for spreading the heavy trail legs and to perform other such tasks. The M-68 is the same weapon as that carried on the self-propelled L-33 mentioned above. These large 155-mm (6.1-in) howitzers are normally towed by 6×6 trucks that also carry the ammunition and the crews, which may be as large as eight men.

The next smallest-calibre towed weapon is an ex-Soviet gun, the 130-mm (5.1-in) M-46 field gun. This is generally regarded as an excellent weapon, and is one of the most widely used guns of its type. Thus when the Israelis captured large numbers in both the 1967 and 1973 campaigns they were only too happy to take them into their own service. They have now gone one stage further, for not only is the ammunition manufactured in Israel specifically for this gun but the basic carriage has been modified to suit local requirements. The original carriage with its single wheel at each end of the axle has been converted into a new version with two wheels on each side attached to the axle by a rocking beam. The M-46 has a range of 29,690 yards

Soltam L-33 155-mm self-propelled gun

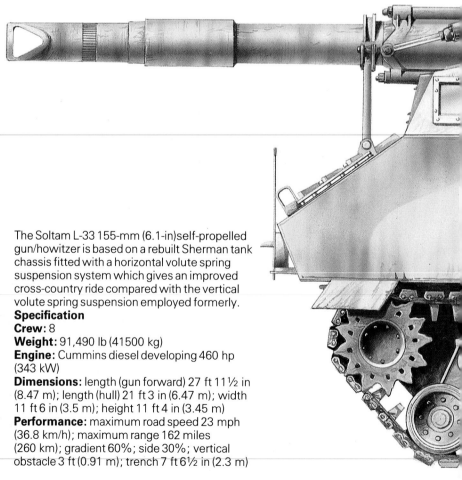

The Soltam L-33 155-mm (6.1-in) self-propelled gun/howitzer is based on a rebuilt Sherman tank chassis fitted with a horizontal volute spring suspension system which gives an improved cross-country ride compared with the vertical volute spring suspension employed formerly.

Specification
Crew: 8
Weight: 91,490 lb (41500 kg)
Engine: Cummins diesel developing 460 hp (343 kW)
Dimensions: length (gun forward) 27 ft 11½ in (8.47 m); length (hull) 21 ft 3 in (6.47 m); width 11 ft 6 in (3.5 m); height 11 ft 4 in (3.45 m)
Performance: maximum road speed 23 mph (36.8 km/h); maximum range 162 miles (260 km); gradient 60%; side 30%; vertical obstacle 3 ft (0.91 m); trench 7 ft 6½ in (2.3 m)

Soltam 155-mm M-68 gun/howitzer

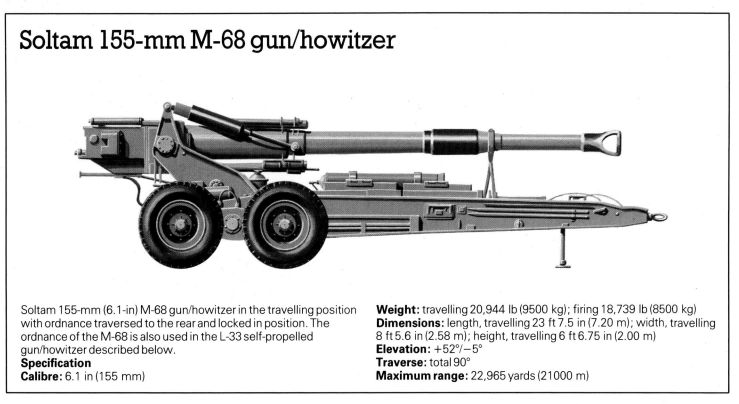

Soltam 155-mm (6.1-in) M-68 gun/howitzer in the travelling position with ordnance traversed to the rear and locked in position. The ordnance of the M-68 is also used in the L-33 self-propelled gun/howitzer described below.

Specification
Calibre: 6.1 in (155 mm)

Weight: travelling 20,944 lb (9500 kg); firing 18,739 lb (8500 kg)
Dimensions: length, travelling 23 ft 7.5 in (7.20 m); width, travelling 8 ft 5.6 in (2.58 m); height, travelling 6 ft 6.75 in (2.00 m)
Elevation: +52°/−5°
Traverse: total 90°
Maximum range: 22,965 yards (21000 m)

D-30 122-mm howitzer

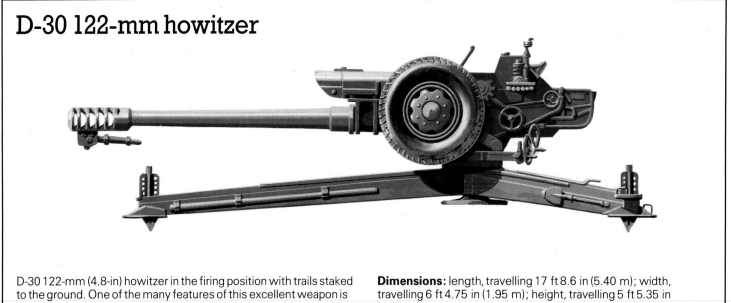

D-30 122-mm (4.8-in) howitzer in the firing position with trails staked to the ground. One of the many features of this excellent weapon is that it can be quickly traversed through 360 degrees without moving the carriage.

Specification

Calibre: 4.8 in (121.92 mm)

Weight: travelling 7,077 lb (3210 kg); firing 6,944 lb (3150 kg)

Dimensions: length, travelling 17 ft 8.6 in (5.40 m); width, travelling 6 ft 4.75 in (1.95 m); height, travelling 5 ft 5.35 in (1.66 m)

Elevation: +70°/−7°

Traverse: 360°

Maximum range: with HE projectile 16,840 yards (15400 m) and with HE rocket-assisted projectile 22,965 yards (21000 m)

(27150 m) and fires a projectile weighing 74 lb (33.5 kg). Because of its size it requires a crew of nine, and is heavy enough at a travelling weight of 18,630-lb (8450 kg) to require a specialist tractor.

Another weapon that has entered the Israeli gun park as a form of war booty is the ex-Soviet 122-mm (4.8-in) D-30 howitzer. This is another example of Soviet artillery design excellence that has been distributed worldwide, for it is a long-barrelled howitzer emplaced on a field carriage that allows 360° traverse. The carriage has three trail legs that fold together for transport and open up to form a flat tripod over which the howitzer can traverse. The equipment also has a useful range of 16,840 yards (15400 m) and fires a projectile weighing 48 lb (21.7 kg). The ammunition fired is

largely the same as that used by another ex-Soviet howitzer, the 122-mm (4.8-in) Model 1938, or M-30. This is also in Israeli hands as the result of war gains but the Model 1938 is a much older and more conventional weapon than the D-30, and the majority of those now in Israeli service are used only for training.

Smaller veteran

The smallest of the artillery calibres in service is 105 mm (4.13 in). There now remains only one type of weapon of this size in service, the 105-mm (4.13-in) M101 howitzer, and only some 70 of these now remain in use. The M101 is a venerable piece of ordnance that can trace its American origins back to 1920, when it was originally known as the M2. Over the years

A Soltam 155-mm (6.1-in) M-71 gun/howitzer in the firing position, with projectiles in the foreground. The main difference between this and the M-68 is that the M-71 has a longer 39-calibre barrel, and therefore a longer range.

M-64 130-mm field gun

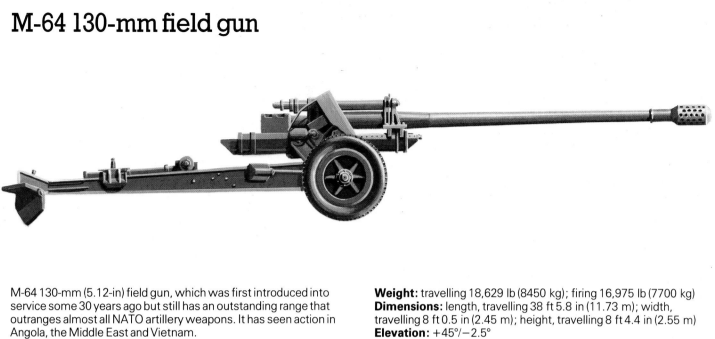

M-64 130-mm (5.12-in) field gun, which was first introduced into service some 30 years ago but still has an outstanding range that outranges almost all NATO artillery weapons. It has seen action in Angola, the Middle East and Vietnam.

Specification
Calibre: 5.12 in (130 mm)

Weight: travelling 18,629 lb (8450 kg); firing 16,975 lb (7700 kg)
Dimensions: length, travelling 38 ft 5.8 in (11.73 m); width, travelling 8 ft 0.5 in (2.45 m); height, travelling 8 ft 4.4 in (2.55 m)
Elevation: +45°/−2.5°
Traverse: total 50°
Maximum range: 29,690 yards (27150 m)

changes have been made, but they have been slight and the M101 remains a sturdy and reliable field howitzer. Its use is now confined largely to reserve units. At one time there was a self-propelled version of this gun in Israeli service. This was the M7, but none now remains as their chassis have been either scrapped or converted for other uses.

In Israel artillery includes mortars, and the IDF/A uses these on quite a large scale. The mortars include a large Soltam 160-mm (6.3-in) mortar, which is normally carried on a converted Sherman or M7 chassis and is often included in tank brigades as the main weapon of the artillery battalion. It is a good counter-battery weapon for use against multiple rocket-launchers and is also a good weapon for use in built-up areas. The bomb fired by the 160-mm (6.3-in) mortar weighs 88 lb (40 kg) and the range is 10,500 yards (9600 m). Each self-propelled mortar carrier can carry 56 bombs.

When used as a towed weapon the 160-mm (6.3-in) mortar is a heavy load and requires a crew of up to eight men.

The 120-mm (4.72-in) mortar may also be used in either a self-propelled or a towed manner. On the self-propelled version the mortar is carried on a special carriage inside a M113 carrier and fires through the roof hatches. On tow it can be pulled by light vehicles such as Jeeps. The range of the 120-mm (4.72-in) mortar is about 7,100 yards (6500 m) and most bombs fired weigh about 28.66 lb (13 kg). The normal in-service version of the 120-mm (4.72-in) mortar is the M-65, but there is also a special light version.

While dealing with guns it would be as well to mention the anti-aircraft guns in use. Calibres in this category do not rise above 40 mm, for above that calibre missiles tend to be more efficient. The 40-mm anti-aircraft gun involved is the venerable Bofors, a

A captured Soviet supplied 122-mm (4.8-in) D-30 gun/howitzer used by the IDF/A with projectile and charge in the foreground. Note the towing eye folded back under the forward part of the barrel.

A TCM-20 twin 20-mm anti-aircraft gun system in travelling configuration. This system is credited with shooting down 10 aircraft in 10 engagements during the War of Attrition.

weapon that is still very efficient in the anti-aircraft role despite its age. The guns in Israeli use include both the old ex-American L/60 guns and the more modern L/70 guns (the 'L' number denotes the length of the barrel in calibres). These guns are mounted on field carriages that provide 360° traverse, and they are effective up to about 10,000 ft (3050 m).

Next down the calibre scale is the Soviet 23-mm ZU-23 anti-aircraft gun. These may be mounted on field carriages either in pairs or mounted together in fours. In either case they are very effective against low-flying aircraft, even travelling at speed. The twin guns have a cyclic fire rate of up to 2,000 rpm and the quadruple mountings can produce a theoretical rate of fire of 2,400 rpm or more.

This rate of fire tends to pale somewhat when the American 20-mm 'Gatling' guns are considered. Again, two types are in Israeli service, a self-propelled version and a towed version. The self-propelled version is the M163 20-mm Vulcan anti-aircraft gun system, which is carried in a modified M113 armoured personnel carrier. The gun is partially controlled by an onboard radar system and the single gun carried can produce a rate of fire of 1,000 or 3,000 rpm. The barrels rotate about a central pivot and each of the six barrels involved is progressively loaded, fired and cleared as it rotates. The towed version is the M167, identical in most respects to the self-propelled version other than that it uses a towed carriage mounted on a single axle. In both cases the gun is controlled by a single man with another acting as a target spotter and fire-control assistant. The towed version is light enough to be carried by a light 4×4 truck.

The Israelis also make a great deal of use of 20-mm aircraft cannon mounted on ex-American quadruple gun mountings that originally carried 0.5-in (12.7-mm) Browning M2 heavy machine-guns. Each quadruple mounting now carries two 20-mm Hispano Suiza HS 404 cannon with a combined rate of fire of over 1,300 rpm. This new carriage/cannon combination is known as the TCM-20 and is produced in both towed and self-propelled versions, the self-propelled version being carried on a half-track. In service this has proved to be a very successful weapon and is now being produced for export to several other countries.

The use of some of these mortars and anti-aircraft guns is not confined to the Artillery Corps, and the weapons may be found in use with some of the other corps.

The Infantry

In the IDF/A the infantry generally speaking rides into battle on wheels or tracks. In the mechanized infantry brigades and battalions the armoured personnel carrier (APC) is the normal mode of travel, while in other infantry formations half-tracks or other APCs are used, and at the very least the soldiers move about in trucks.

It would be safe to say that the IDF/A has refined the use of the APC to new height and also moved it into new tactical areas. Many armies still tend to regard the APC as a form of 'battle taxi' in which the troops are carried into battle, where they dismount. The IDF/A, on the other hand, regards the APC as a vehicle from which troops can fight. Thus the Israeli infantryman looks on his APC as base, carrying in and on it all his kit

A TCM-20 twin 20-mm anti-aircraft
gun system deployed in the field. This
is essentially an old American M55
system, with the original four
12.7-mm (0.5-in) M2 MGs replaced by
two 20-mm cannon.

A TCM-20 twin 20-mm anti-aircraft
gun system with an Israeli designed
and built EL/M-2106 point defence
alerting radar in the background. The
radar warns the gunner of the
approach of enemy aircraft.

TCM-20 self-propelled 20-mm twin anti-aircraft gun

Half-track of the Israel Defence Force/Army fitted with the RAMTA Structures and Systems twin 20 mm TCM-20 anti-aircraft gun system. Each 20-mm cannon is fitted with a drum type magazine holding 60 rounds of ammunition. Traverse is electric through 360 degrees while elevation is electric from −10 degrees to +90 degrees. Maximum effective range when being used in the anti-aircraft role is about 1,312 yards (1200m) and 1,640 yards (1500 m) in the ground-to-ground role. Each 20-mm cannon has a practical rate of fire of 150 rounds per minute.

Left: IDF/A half-track fitted with the TCM-20 twin 20-mm anti-aircraft gun system in action on the Golan Heights. Although developed for the anti-aircraft role, it was also used in the ground role during the 1973 war.

and equipment and the support weapons he will use once fighting commences. He only dismounts when the tactical situation demands such an action. This goes a long way to explaining the generally cluttered appearance of most Israeli APCs. Each vehicle, whatever its type, is covered with extra racks and equipment, and heavy machine-guns cover the roof.

For many years in the IDF/A the APC meant the venerable half-track, the old American M2 or M3. When the IDF/A was gathering together weapons and equipment during the 1950s it obtained as many half-tracks from as many sources as was possible. That even meant purchasing hulks from scrapyards as far afield as the Philippines, but once in Israel these relics were extensively refurbished and put into use. More

came from the USA, France and the United Kingdom. Today many are still in use, although many others have been replaced by the M113. The half-tracks are still in use as ambulances, control and command posts, anti-aircraft mountings carrying the TCM-20, anti-tank guns carrying a 106-mm (4.17-in) recoilless rifle, mortar carrier carrying 81-mm or 120-mm mortars, artillery fire-control vehicle, ammunition and supplies carrier, and so on. As a personnel carrier the half-track can carry a crew of two and a section of eight men. All the half-tracks in service today have been reconditioned for the umpteenth time, and now have diesel engines and extra weapon mountings. It seems they will remain in service for years to come.

Outside the United States the largest operator of the

M113 tracked APC is Israel, where the IDF/A has well over 4,000 of the type with yet another 800 to be delivered. The M113 has now largely replaced the half-track as the standard APC of the IDF/A, and the M113 has also received the usual Israeli accolade of being festooned with extra racks and equipment. The M113 has even received a name, the soldiers calling it the *Zelda*. As a personnel carrier the M113 has a crew of two and the capacity to carry up to 11 men with their equipment, but in some Israeli units this load is reduced in order to make long-term occupation more bearable. The M113 is also used for many special purposes. It is used as a mortar carrier for both 81-mm and 120-mm mortars, and may be seen fitted with TOW anti-tank missile-launchers on the roof. A front-line ambulance version is in service, and there are some variations on the front-line workshops and repair vehicle theme. The Israelis have also made their own modifications to suit their own peculiar requirements. There is little chance that their M113s will ever be called upon to cross sizable water obstacles, so the standard trim vanes have been removed altogether, and the exhausts have been re-routed to prevent the fumes entering the interior when the roof hatches are open as they usually are in the Palestine climate. The number of weapon mountings on the roof has also been increased to up to four, each of which can carry either a 7.62-mm or a 12.7-mm (0.3-in or 0.5-in) machine-gun.

The IDF/A also uses three types of Soviet APCs, all of them captured during the campaigns against Syria and Egypt. These are the BTR-40, BTR-50 and BTR-60. The smallest is the 4×4 BTR-40, a wheeled APC carrying a crew of two and a section of eight men. In appearance

it resembles a wheeled truck. The BTR-50 is tracked and uses the chassis of the Soviet PT-76 light tank, small numbers of which serve with some Israeli reconnaissance units. It is a much larger vehicle than the BTR-40 and can carry a crew of two and up to 20 men in a box superstructure. There is a Czech version of this vehicle known as the OT-62, and the IDF/A uses numbers of these also. The BTR-60 is wheeled and has a full 8×8 drive and suspension system. It can carry a crew of two and up to 16 men at a squeeze. All three of these APCs can carry a machine-gun armament and have some

An M113 fitted with an experimental two-man turret, armed with Israel Military Industries 60-mm Hyper-velocity Medium Support Weapons (HVMS), which can fire an HE or APFSDS-T round.

A Sherman tank chassis rebuilt by Soltam and fitted with a 160-mm (6.3-in) breech-loaded mortar. When in the firing position the forward part of the superstructure folds down horizontally, to give more room.

The American M113 APC is used in large numbers to transport infantry on the battlefield, and is commonly known as the Zelda. Most have additional machine-guns installed on the roof.

amphibious capabilities. They are mainly used by the reserve formations.

Two other types of ex-Soviet APC remain to be mentioned. The IDF/A does use quite large numbers of the BTR-152 APC, which may be conveniently regarded as a 6×6 version of the BTR-40. Numerous versions of this vehicle exist, many of them in Israeli service, and ranging from command posts to fully-enclosed special signals vehicles. As an APC the BTR-152 can carry a crew of two and up to 17 men, although less have to be carried for them to be comfortable. The BTR-152 has several attractions for the Israelis. One is the variable tyre pressure system, which has been widely copied on other designs, and the other is the general handiness and cross-country performance of

the vehicle. The design has so impressed some Israeli vehicle experts that they have produced their own design based on the BTR-152. This vehicle has definite visual similarities with the Soviet original: it is known as the Shoet 11 and has been produced primarily for the export market, though there are indications that the Shoet might have already been taken into IDF/A use.

The last APC that must be mentioned is the Egyptian Walid. In many ways the Walid resembles a Soviet BTR-40 but its armoured superstructure is based on a West German Magirus Deutz chassis. Large numbers of Walids fell into Israeli hands in 1967, and since that time they have been used by the various border infantry and other such battalions as their standard APC. The Walid can carry a driver and up to 10 men,

Israeli infantrymen dismount from their M113 armoured personnel carrier via the power-operated ramp in the hull rear. The basic vehicle is armed with a 12.7-mm (0.5-in) machine gun, although additional 7.62 (0.31-in) machine-guns are normally fitted.

M113 used as an engineer vehicle by the IDF/A, with barbed wire on hull front. Note the rearranged exhaust pipe that stops fumes blowing back into the crew compartment.

The new 9-mm Mini-Uzi sub-machine-gun, with the stock extended for ready use. It can be fitted with 20, 25 or 32 round capacity magazines, and is said to have a cyclic rate of fire of 1,200 rpm.

but it has an open top and is thus vulnerable to artillery fire. Some Walids are used by the Israelis as stores and ammunition carriers.

The personal weapons of the Israeli soldier have in recent years settled down to a relatively orderly mixture, a useful improvement over the situation in the early years when any type of weapon that could be obtained was on issue. It is still possible to find some rather ancient weapons in use with the home-defence groups, but these pages deal only with the main weapons used.

The smallest of them is the 9-mm Beretta Model 51 automatic pistol which can hold eight rounds in the butt. It is issued to officers and some specialist troops such as the military police.

Next up the scale is the Uzi sub-machine gun, one of the success stories of the Israeli defence industry for it still attracts export orders even though it has been in production since the early 1950s. It is a 9-mm weapon that is short and handy, and it may be fitted with either a folding or a fixed stock. The magazines hold either 25 or 32 rounds, and the overall design has earned for itself an enviable reputation for reliability and ease of handling. The Uzi is used widely throughout the IDF/A and is issued to tank crews, paratroops and many other such non-infantry units. A new version, the Mini-Uzi, is now in production and is being issued to specialists such as bodyguards and security personnel. It is smaller than the standard Uzi and weighs only 5.95 lb (2.7 kg) complete.

An Israeli Military Industries 9-mm UZI sub-machine gun, with the metal stock in the unfolded position and the additional box-type magazine alongside. The latter can hold 25 or 32 rounds of ammunition.

With rifles the situation is a trifle more complex. The general impression given is that the Israeli Galil is the standard weapon, but this is not strictly correct. The Galil is issued to the front-line formations in both 5.56-mm and 7.62-mm forms, but it is not the only rifle in service. The others are the Belgian FN FAL in 7.62-mm calibre, the American 5.56-mm M16A1 and large numbers of captured ex-Soviet AK-47s and AKMs.

The Galil is another of the defence industry's success stories, for the design has been exported and adopted widely. There are indications that the design sprang from a derivative of the Soviet AK-47, but the Israelis claim that it is an original design which is now produced and used in several versions. The larger versions are fitted with a folding butt and a bipod, but the shorter versions are designed for use rather like a sub-machine gun and so do not have the bipod. Both 7.62-mm and 5.56-mm versions are produced. There is even a superbly-engineered sniper rifle version which can be fitted with a variety of special sights. Odd features include the fact that the bipod incorporates a wire cutter, a bottle opener is built in to prevent soldiers wrecking more sensitive parts of the rifle when opening pop bottles, and the muzzle has a special built-in adapter to enable it to fire rifle grenades. A recent innovation is a semi-transparent plastic magazine that enables the user to see how much ammunition is left at any particular stage.

However, the Galil is not the only front-line rifle for, as mentioned above, large numbers of the Belgian FN FAL (Fusil Automatique Léger) are in use. This is a 7.62-mm rifle virtually identical to similar rifles used throughout NATO. It has a box magazine holding 20 rounds.

When the Americans started to supply Israel with weapons and other equipment the benefits included a supply of 5.56-mm M16A1 rifles, the standard US Army rifle that is commonly known as the Armalite. These light rifles have been issued mainly to such specialist units as the paratroops where its handiness and overall lightness are best appreciated. The M16A1 can be fitted with either a 20- or a 30-round magazine, and it can be used to fire light grenades. For this purpose special underslung 40-mm grenade-launchers are carried under the barrel, and these have a range of up to 440 yards (400 m).

The AK-47 and its later derivative, the AKM, have both come to the IDF/A by way of war booty. They are not, generally speaking, issued to front-line units but are held in reserve and are used by local militias and home-defence groups. They are excellent weapons that fire a short 7.62-mm cartridge.

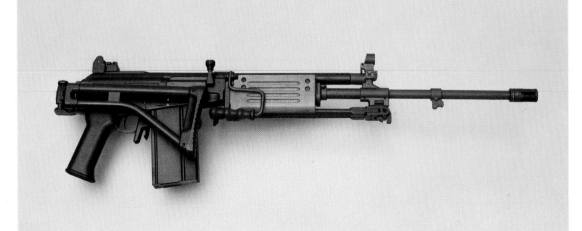

A 5.56-mm Galil assault rifle, with the metal stock folded alongside. The Galil can be fitted with quickly detachable magazines holding 12, 35 or 50 rounds of ammunition.

A Galil 5.56-mm assault rifle, with a folding metal stock and fitted with a bipod showing various attachments including the three types of magazine, rifle grenades and bayonet and scabbard. The Galil can also be fitted with a telescopic sight.

With machine-guns there are no local designs, but the FN MAG general-purpose machine-guns were made locally and are now the standard machine-guns for the infantry. They use a belt feed and fire the usual 7.62-mm NATO cartridge. Their rate of fire may be as high as 1,000 rpm and they can be used at ranges of up to 1,300 yards (1200 m). The type may be used either from a light bipod for the infantry role or mounted on a heavy tripod in the sustained-fire role. Another FN machine-gun is the light FN FAL fitted with a heavy barrel and a bipod. This is used as a section support weapon and is not suitable for the sustained-fire role.

Most vehicles carry at least one 0.3-in (7.62-mm) Browning machine-gun. This is an air-cooled belt-fed weapon, and although it has been in use since 1919 in the United States it is still an excellent weapon. It has a rate of fire of up to 500 rpm. Another Browning machine-gun is used in the heavy role, namely the venerable Browning 0.5-in (12.7-mm) M2. Over the years this weapon has proved to be one of the finest weapons of its type ever designed, and it is still in production after being around for over 50 years. Most of the M2s are carried on vehicles, but the type can be fired from a ground tripod. It has an effective range of well over 1,100 yards (1000 m) and is still a good anti-aircraft weapon. The rate of fire is up to 650 rpm.

A small selection of the huge amount of small arms captured by the IDF/A during the invasion of Lebanon in 1982. Most of this equipment came from Warsaw Pact countries, especially the Soviet Union, although some Western arms were found.

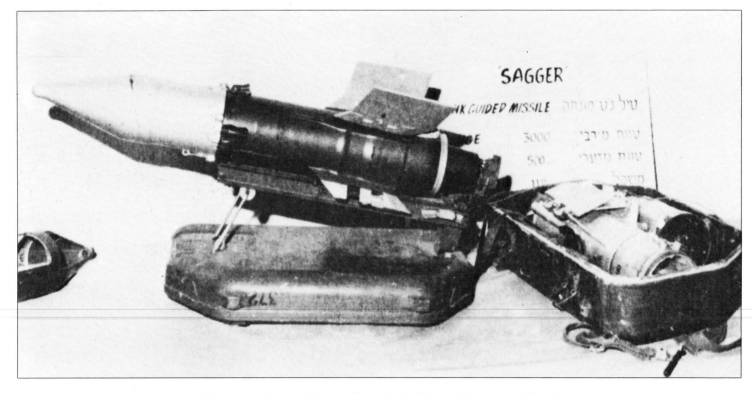

SAGGER

IK GUIDED MISSILE

טיל נ"ט מונחה

טווח מירבי 3000

טווח מזערי 500

A Soviet-supplied Sagger ATGW in its basic man-portable infantry version, which was used in large numbers by Egypt and Syria in the 1973 conflict.

For general fire support the Israeli infantry makes much use of mortars and the smallest is used at platoon level in the form of the portable 52-mm IMI mortar. A local design, the 52-mm mortar has a possible range of 460 yards (420 m) and fires a small bomb weighing 2.3 lb (1.05 kg). It can fire up to 25 of these every minute.

The normal company mortar is the 81-mm Soltam mortar, which may be issued in either long-barrel or short-barrel versions. Normally these are carried into action by a team of three men. Using special long-range ammunition these mortars can reach out to 7100 yards (6500 m) and can fire HE, smoke and illuminating bombs. In some mechanized formations these mortars are carried in M113 APCs.

For anti-tank use at company level the IDF/A still relies mainly on the 84-mm Carl Gustav, a Swedish recoilless gun. This weapon fires a projectile that weighs 5.7 lb (2.6 kg) and can penetrate up to 15.75 in (400 m) of armour under ideal conditions. However, as

it has a calibre of only 84 mm, it is now considered at best obsolescent and is due to be replaced.

Its replacement is still a matter for conjecture, for several types of short-range anti-tank missile have been tried. Two of them have been tried locally as they are home-designed products. These are the B-300 and the Picket, both shoulder-launched weapons that are theoretically capable of defeating most current MBTs. If fired against the thinner armour of most future MBTs they would undoubtedly be able to penetrate it, but the frontal armour would probably be invulnerable. Thus although small numbers of B-300s and Pickets may be in service they are unlikely to be used in large numbers.

Anti-tank defence would therefore appear to be invested in higher command levels. Two anti-tank missile systems are already in widespread service in the IDF/A, namely Dragon and TOW. Dragon has a range of only about 1,100 yards (1000 m) and relies for inflight correction on a series of miniature rocket

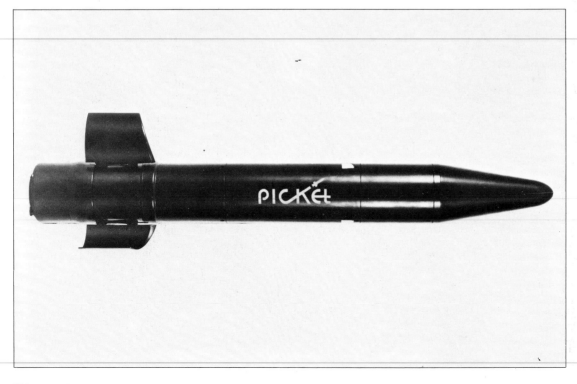

Picket is a shoulder-launched infantry anti-tank missile developed in Israel, and small numbers may be in army service. Each round consists of the missile packed in a disposable launcher tube.

Far right: A captured Soviet-supplied BMP-1 mechanized infantry fighting vehicle, with 'Sagger' ATGW above the 73-mm gun. This vehicle was used by Egypt and Syria in the 1973 war.

motors set along the sides of the body which ignite to 'kick' the missile onto its correct flight path. Inflight corrections are sent to the missile along a wire that trails from the missile, the aimer using a light weapon stand to steady the missile launch tube and the fire-control sight unit. When not in use against armour the Dragon makes an excellent 'bunker-buster' for it can penetrate 3 ft (0.91 m) of concrete.

The TOW is in another class, for it is a much heavier weapon than the Dragon with a maximum range of up to 4,100 yards (3750 m). It can also knock out almost any tank it is fired against, with the exception of the very latest Soviet tanks, and even then improvements to the missile, which the Israelis will no doubt adopt, may remedy this situation. TOW is an optically-guided missile that receives its inflight guidance corrections automatically via a trailed wire. Compared with other such missiles it is a relatively fast missile and when used by a properly trained 'gunner' it is very accurate. TOW can be fired from a heavy tripod, but to make maximum use of its effectiveness the Israelis usually carry the type mounted on M113 APCs or other vehicles such as light Jeeps. The first TOW missiles arrived in Israel during the 1973 war and have remained in use ever since. More are currently on order.

The above outline of current IDF/A equipment is not comprehensive, for the Israelis continually strive to improve current weapons and to introduce new ones, the Blazer active armour being a case in point. They constantly have to keep up this use of technology to replace manpower, for the number of men who can serve in the IDF/A is finite and it would now appear that the number of people who can usefully reside and work in Israel has been reached and that the fragile economic structure cannot withstand any more large-scale social impositions. Thus advanced technology has to replace numbers and many of the current weapon systems in prospect or already in service are what could be termed 'man-multipliers'. The tank is a good example of the latter, for a crew of four men in one tank can command a stretch of terrain that once had to

TOW was first used by Israel in the 1973 war, and has since proved effective against most Soviet-supplied armour. It can be used by infantry, but more usually in Israeli service TOW launchers are mounted on Jeeps or M113 APCs as depicted here.

be occupied physically by large bodies of men.

The IDF/A cannot, however, rely upon technology alone for the future survival of the nation. The IDF/A trains long and it trains hard, to the extent that such training has converted a workers' militia into one of the most capable fighting forces the world has ever seen. The polyglot population has been welded into a force that can fight using complex weapons and tactics that is a wonder to the rest of the military world. Apart from technology and training, the Israelis have one further motivating force: they know that if they ever lose a conflict with their neighbours, all that for which they have lived and worked during the last few generations will vanish as if it had never existed, and a new dark age for the Jewish race will begin.

The Israeli Air Force

The Israeli air force expects only one standard – the best. To meet that standard it has always flown the finest aircraft that can be obtained, and the men and women who service and fly the aircraft are the most dedicated and professional in the world. The Israeli aircraft industry does its best to supply the aircraft, but most still have to be obtained from the USA along with much of the sophisticated electronics that now go with them. This combination of man and machinery has provided Israel with a combat record that is now second to none, but it is a record for which the nation has had to pay dearly, both in terms of casualties and cost.

Left: In a scene symbolic of Jewish resistance to foreign oppression, four McDonnell Douglas F-15 Eagles cross the hilltop fort of Masada where 2,000 years ago the defenders committed suicide rather than submit to the might of Rome.

Below: This aircraft is believed to have been the first definitely IAI Kfir-C2, with the added canards and other new features. It proved to be dramatically superior to the Mirage 5 from which it was derived.

Unquestionably the most regularly battle-tested air arm in the world, the Israel Defence Force/Air Force has proved its unparalleled effectiveness in numerous air conflicts and actions, large and small, and gained the grudging respect of even the most bitter of its enemies. Equipped with some of the most potent of today's combat aircraft, it is the key component of the Israel Defence Force and the embodiment of the Jewish people's firm resolve never again to be dispossessed of the land it claims as its birthright.

Here, though, is the reason for the IDF/AF's expertise in air warfare, for the Palestinian Arabs also regard the land on which Israel stands as their own, and they have powerful allies bordering the Jewish state. Four times (in 1948, 1956, 1967 and 1973) the world has held its

breath whilst Israel was locked in combat with its sworn enemies, and more recently, in 1982, the IDF/AF played a decisive role in the thrust into Lebanon in a bid to excise the Palestine Liberation Organization.

Not all of these wars have seen Israel cast in the role of innocent victim of aggression. Arab countries have made no secret of their hostility, but having been almost strangled at birth, Israel has grown up into a master of the pre-emptive strike. The Suez conflict of 1956 was a pre-arranged and ill-starred affair in conjunction with the UK and France, the two Western countries hoping to regain possession of the Suez Canal summarily nationalized by Egypt.

In the Six Day War of 1967, Israel gained a spectacular success against Egypt, Jordan, Syria and Lebanon

The Israeli Air Force

by a first strike, and considerably increased its territory as a result, while the Yom Kippur War of 1973 witnessed a complete reversal. In this case, Israel was caught off its guard by a well-prepared Arab attack, and only frantic action by the IDF/AF and surface forces saved the country from annihilation.

Having survived this onslaught by the narrowest of margins, Israel entered a period of extreme militancy under the recently-retired Prime Minister Menachim Begin, reacting savagely to the slightest provocation by its neighbours. This culminated in the 1982 invasion of southern Lebanon, when the wounding in a gun attack of the Israeli ambassador to London launched an armoured thrust towards Beirut. In this conflict, the IDF/AF imposed a crushing defeat on its Syrian counterpart, but victory was overshadowed by world opinion which firmly pronounced Israel as the aggressor.

Modern equipment

The strong fighting spirit of the IDF/AF has been a major factor in its successes, although determination can offset the disadvantage of inferior numbers only to a certain extent. Thus, Israel has always sought the most effective combat aircraft for its forces, the majority now coming from the United States. Leading the interceptor arm are three squadrons of General Dynamics F-16 Fighting Falcons (plus enough for three more squadrons on order) and two (with another to form) of McDonnell Douglas F-15 Eagles, both of these being up-to-date types with sophisticated weapon systems. A further three units fly the indigenous Israel Aircraft Industries Kfir, which is an adaptation of the Dassault Mirage with a US engine and local improvements including canards and new avionics.

No less effective, the fighter-bomber force relies largely on the sturdy McDonnell Douglas F-4 Phantom, equipping five squadrons, together with a single unit of Kfirs, while for close-support work, another McDonnell Douglas product, the A-4 Skyhawk, continues to give sterling service in four squadrons, again augmented by

Standard SAM for the defence of IDF/AF airbases, the Improved HAWK is seen here on its triple launcher. Missiles are US-supplied; there are no links with NATO European production.

a Kfir unit. In even closer collaboration with the army are three squadrons of Bell AH-1 Cobra helicopter gunships and one of Hughes 500 Defenders, the heavy-lift Sikorsky CH-53s and Aérospatiale SA 321 Super Frelons looking after transport requirements.

Though a small country (the size of Wales if its annexed territories are excluded), Israel maintains a comparatively large fixed-wing transport arm, operating Lockheed C-130 Hercules, Boeing 707 and Douglas C-47 Dakota aircraft. Hercules and Model 707 machines also act as inflight-refuelling tankers, and

All IDF/AF Hughes Model 500MDs appear to have a service number in the 200 range. They have tubes for four TOW missiles, a nose-mounted sight and a 'Black Hole Ocarina' IR-suppressed engine jetpipe.

Israel Aircraft Industries (Fouga) C.170 Magister

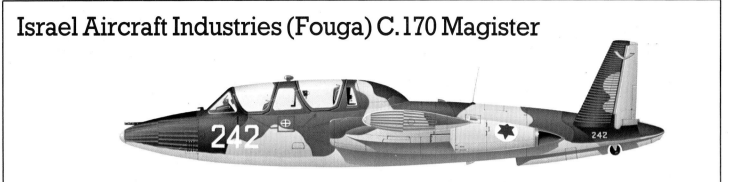

The Fouga Magister was the first type of aircraft ever to be assembled, and later almost entirely manufactured, in Israel. The licence was obtained in December 1956, but it was 7 July 1960 before the lusty infant then named Bedek Aviation, and today called Israel Aircraft Industries, was able to hand over the first aircraft. This example shows the twin 0.3-in (7.62-mm) nose guns which were previously fitted to Israeli Magisters along with other stores.

Specification
Fouga C.M.170 Magister
Type: two-seat jet trainer
Powerplant: two 882-lb (400-kg) thrust Turboméca Marboré IIA turbojets
Performance: maximum speed 403 mph (650 km/h) at sea level,
444 mph (715 km/h) at 30,000 ft (9145 m); initial climb rate 3,345 ft (1020 m) per minute; service ceiling 36,090 ft (11000 m); range (30 ft/9145 m, with reserve) 575 miles (925 km)
Weights: empty 4,740 lb (2150 kg); maximum take-off 7,055 lb (3200 kg)
Dimensions: span (over tanks) 39 ft 10 in (12.15 m); length 33 ft 0 in (10.06 m); height 9 ft 2 in (2.80 m); wing area 186.1 sq ft (17.30 m^2)
Armament: provision for two rifle-calibre machine-guns (0.3-in/7.62-mm) in nose with 200-round boxes; underwing racks may be fitted for two Matra 181 launchers (each 18 rockets of 37-mm calibre), two 110-lb (50-kg) bombs, two AS.11 missiles or two 55-lb (25-kg) air-to-surface rockets

specially-equipped Model 707s perform intelligence-gathering and other electronic tasks, supported by Grumman EV-1E Mohawks, Beech RC-12Ds and IAI Aravas. In a category of its own is the Grumman E-2 Hawkeye with its large parasol-type radome providing early warning and co-ordinating defensive and offensive missions.

The lighter workhorses are the Bell 205, 212 and OH-58 Kiowa helicopters, together with fixed-wing Dornier Do 27s, Do 28s and various Cessnas. Pilot training is undertaken on the Aérospatiale Magister, with Piper Super Cubs providing the initial few hours of instruction.

This predominance of US equipment has not always been the case. The IDF/AF was formed on 10 November 1947 (before the formal creation of Israel) as Shin Aleph, the air arm of the Jewish underground or Haganah, and by the time that Israel was proclaimed as a sovereign state on 14 May 1948, it had 54 aircraft of assorted types. These were thrown into battle on 15

May when Arab forces attacked the day-old country.

A desperate need for additional air equipment brought second-hand aircraft to Israel from far and wide, and numerous are the tales of aircraft (particularly of the ex-military variety) mysteriously disappearing from Europe and the USA only to materialize in Israeli service. Some sympathetic governments turned a blind eye to these events, or even contributed aircraft of their own, but the major driving force was the Jews spread throughout the world. Though they wished to remain in the country of their adoption, their concern for the future of Israel was no less than if they had been living there. This was the first occasion on which expatriate Jews had the opportunity to aid their homeland; it was not to be the last.

The French connection
During the 1950s, France emerged as a major supplier of aircraft to the IDF/AF, providing Dassault Mystère IVAs, Dassault Super Mystère B.2s, Dassault Ouragans and Sud-Ouest Vautour IIA/IINs for the

For many years the McDonnell Douglas A-4 Skyhawk has been one of the most important Israeli combat types. This A-4E has the camel-hump avionics, but lacks the extended jetpipe added in the 1970s.

Since backed up by the Sikorsky S-65, the Aérospatiale Super Frelon was Israel's first large transport helicopter, supplied in both amphibious and (as here) tactical versions. The engines were changed to GE T58s to improve performance.

combat squadrons, plus Nord Noratlas transports and Fouga Magister trainers. A licence was obtained for local assembly of the Magister by Bedek Aircraft, and when the first was handed over to the IDF/AF in 1960, it marked the beginning of aircraft manufacture in Israel.

Ever eager to obtain advanced aircraft, the IDF/AF was an early customer for the Dassault Mirage III, and this aircraft played a prominent part in the Six Day War of 1967, both as an interceptor and fighter-bomber. Well pleased with its performance, Israel contracted for a batch of 50 simplified Mirage 5s, but swayed by Arab political pressure, France placed an embargo on their delivery and the aircraft remained in storage for some years until allocated to the French air force.

The void created by withdrawal of French support was rapidly filled by the United States, as evidenced by the Skyhawks, Phantoms, Eagles and Fighting Falcons now forming the backbone of the combat element. The USA has also taken on the role of Israel's main economic supporter in view of the crippling burden of defence spending on the national economy.

In 1984, for example, the USA provided $1,700 million-worth of military equipment, half of it an outright gift, and a further $850 million in economic assistance.

One of the advantages to the US of supplying Israel with its best combat aircraft is the feed-back it obtains on the operational performance of equipment in battle. Syria, now the principal Arab opponent to Israel, is largely equipped with Soviet arms, whose operational strengths and weaknesses are of vital interest to the USA. Israel has also been able to report on various aspects of US weapon performance, and doubtless its assessments have influenced the development of American combat aircraft.

The USA has also played a significant part in Israel's political life, one of its major achievements being the organization of the rapprochement with Egypt at the Camp David summit. This removed Egypt as a military opponent to Israel, in exchange for additional sums of aid to both parties and the handing back to Egypt of territory in the Sinai Desert. The USA replaced, largely at its own cost, two air bases which Israel had to evacuate in Sinai.

Usually based at the pilot training school at Hatzerim, these four Fouga Magisters are part of the IDF/AF national aerobatic team. They are painted blue and white, retaining the badge of two flamingoes.

The two-seat IAI Kfir-TC2 serves both as an advanced trainer, with weapons capability, and also in the electronic-warfare role. Like most Kfirs they are now painted in air-superiority grey overall.

An impressive array of stores can be carried by the Kfir-C2, including 30-mm guns, bombs of up to 3,000 lb (1361 kg) rockets and AAMs. Since this display the surface-attack capability has been enhanced by Maverick, Hobos, Shrike and Gabriel missiles.

to cancel the strategic co-operation agreement, which has not yet been reinstated. This is indeed unusual, for thanks to a strong Jewish lobby in the US legislature, Israel is in the position of 'Uncle Sam's' favourite nephew, and previous embargoes and sanctions imposed by the USA in response to Israeli actions have usually lasted only a few months before being forgotten.

Made in Israel: the Kfir

Though Israel has regularly been able to embarrass the USA by its unilateral actions, safe in the knowledge that it will suffer, at worst, only temporary inconvenience, it remains haunted by the spectre of the French arms cut-off in 1967. Accordingly, considerable effort has been put into indigenous arms manufacture, both for security of supply and the desperately needed foreign currency obtained by export of weapons. Best known of the aircraft in this category is the IAI Kfir, whose resemblance to the Mirage is far from coincidental.

With typical resourcefulness, the IDF/AF decided that if it could not take delivery of the Mirage 5s standing idle in storage at Dassault's plant in France, it would build its own. The first step was, of course, to obtain the necessary drawings to enable IAI to fabricate components, and this was accomplished deviously through an agent in Switzerland. Several crates of blueprints arrived at Lydda (Lod), and IAI was in the Mirage business.

The Camp David agreement significantly increased Israel's security by virtually eliminating the danger of a further war on two fronts, and was followed in November 1981 by an important strategic co-operation agreement. Based largely on the anticipated requirements of the Rapid Deployment Force which the USA was then organizing for intervention in the Middle East, it provided for construction of two new air bases in the Negev Desert; stockpiles of US weapons in Israel; military intelligence sharing and joint operational planning; placing of overhaul contracts with Israeli companies for USAF and US Navy 6th Fleet aircraft; and IAF fighter escort facilities for US transport aircraft overflying the Mediterranean in time of conflict.

The far-reaching implications of this agreement were entirely negated a few days after its conclusion when Israel officially annexed the strategically important Golan Heights area (formerly Syrian land) which it had occupied since the 1967 war. The US reaction was

The initial product was named the Nesher and powered by the SNECMA Atar engine used in the standard Mirage. About 50 Neshers were built and took part in the 1973 war. Later supplanted by Kfirs, they are believed to have been refurbished and sold to Argentina as the Dagger, 36 being supplied in time for participation in the 1982 Falklands war with the UK. The original French-built Mirage IIICJs went in the same direction after the South Atlantic conflict, Argentina taking delivery of 19 plus three trainers from the original 72 and five supplied.

Israel Aircraft Industries Kfir-C2

The IAI Kfir-C2 shown here was the first combat aircraft not only built but also designed in Israel, though derived from an existing French aircraft. Among the changes to accommodate the new engine are enlarged inlets and ducts, a redesigned rear fuselage, internal heat-insulating liner and ram-air cooling inlet in the dorsal fin, and a totally new nose packed with Israeli missile avionics. New aerodynamic features include the dogtooth leading edges, nose strakes and fixed canards above the inlets.

Israel Aircraft Industries Kfir-C2

This Kfir-C2 is one of those subsequently brought up to the current production standard, designated Kfir-C7. This has improved payload/range capability, but to the pilot the chief advantage is its HOTAS (hands on throttle and stick) cockpit controls, the whole cockpit being considerably modernized. The red/white striped rudder may denote No. 101 Sqn.

Specification
Israel Aircraft Industries Kfir-C2
Type: single-seat multi-role fighter
Powerplant: one General Electric (Bet-Shemesh-built) J79-GE-17 afterburning turbojet of 17,860-lb (8020-kg) static thrust
Performance: maximum speed in level flight at altitude 1,650 mph (2655 km/h) or Mach 2.5, at sea level 864 mph (1390 km/h) or

Mach 1.136; climb to 50,053 ft (15250 m) and Mach 2.0 in 4 minutes 30 seconds; service ceiling 59,055 ft (18000 m); radius of action in hi-lo-hi combat air patrol 407 miles (655 km) with 40 minutes on station, in ground attack mission 425-mile (680-km) radius with six 500-lb (227-kg) bombs in hi-lo-hi mission
Weights: air-combat take-off with two Shafrir air-to-air missiles and 50 per cent internal fuel 20,657 lb (9370 kg); maximum take-off 32,121 lb (14570 kg)
Dimensions: span 26 ft 11½ in (8.22 m); length 51 ft 0 in (15.55 m); height 14 ft 11 in (4.55 m); wing area 374.5 sq ft (34.8 m²)
Armament: two 30-mm DEFA cannon with 280 rounds, plus up to 8,818 lb (4000 kg) of external stores on eight hardpoints

Production of the Nesher was limited, because Israel had in mind a complete revision of the Mirage design, the most important feature of which was fitment of the General Electric J79 afterburning turbojet. A two-seat Mirage IIIB tested the new combination in September 1971, and two years later the prototype Kfir was flying. The American engine endowed the 'Mirage' with a much improved performance, but had the disadvantage of giving the US a say in export orders, several potential contracts falling through when Washington exercised its veto. Restrictions have recently been relaxed, resulting in sales to Colombia and Ecuador in 1982.

Externally, the Kfir differs from its progenitor through having a shorter but larger-diameter rear

fuselage tailored to the J79. Closer examination reveals an air scoop in place of the triangular dorsal fin, plus four small fuselage air scoops (for afterburner cooling); a larger, but more flattened undersurface to the forward fuselage; and taller, strengthened landing gear. Internally, the Kfir has increased fuel tankage, a redesigned cockpit and a large proportion of Israeli-built equipment.

The original Kfir was first revealed in April 1975, but a little over a year later, Israel showed a new variant known as the Kfir-C2. This featured detachable canard foreplanes on the air intake ducts, together with extended wing leading edges and small strakes on each side of the nose, their effect being to improve manoeuvrability when dogfighting at relatively low

Shafrir 2 air-to-air missile

First of the important series of air-launched missiles to be developed in Israel, the Shafrir 2 was produced by Rafael Armament Development Authority. It has always been claimed to be much

more effective than early models of AIM-9 Sidewinder, though it operates on broadly similar principles.

Python 3 air-to-air missile

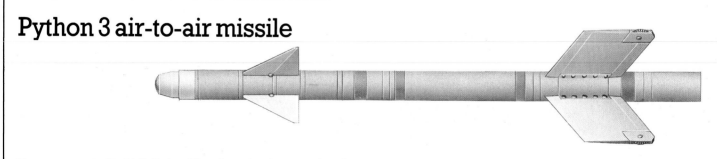

The successor to Shafrir 2, Python 3 is a direct development though with completely new IR homing guidance with 'all-aspect' capability. Able to pull 30g in turns, this more powerful AAM first

went into action over eastern Lebanon in 1983. Rafael ADA state that its performance is similar to that of the latest Sidewinder, AIM-9L, though it has a slightly larger (24.25 lb/11 kg) warhead.

The prominent yellow triangles seen on some of the first Kfirs, and also on many Mirages and Neshers, were adopted to facilitate instant identification – the opposite of camouflage and low-visibility paint. In any case they were copied by the Egyptian air force!

Despite the increased payload and range capability of the Kfir, the off-runway capability has actually been enhanced, with low-pressure tubeless tyres on strengthened long-stroke oleo legs.

speed. Kfir-Cls were updated to this standard and some aircraft have been fitted with an Elta EL/M-2001B radar in an extended nose.

As a replacement for its ageing Mirage IIIBs, the IDF/AF has acquired the Kfir-TC2 tandem-seat trainer, first flown in February 1981. Newest development, however, is the Kfir-C7, which was revealed to be in production during 1983. This has the M-2001 radar as standard for target ranging in conjunction with the new WDNS 341 weapon-delivery and navigation system, and is compatible with the latest laser-guided 'smart' bombs. Take-off weight is increased by 3,395 lb (1540 kg) and overall performance correspondingly improved by a 'Combat +' modification to the J79-J1E which persuades it to give a further 1,000 lb (454 kg) of thrust.

Excluding exports and those lost in service, the IDF/AF has some 180 Kfirs in operation with five squadrons, and will probably take delivery of a further

40 or so before production ends in 1986.

Naturally enough, the Kfir is armed with locally-produced weaponry, beginning with licence-built DEFA 552 30-mm cannon in two internal bays. Under each wing it can carry a Rafael Shafrir or Python AAM for interception, or a Rafael Luz ASM when used in the strike role. The Shafrir is a short-range, infra-red homing dogfight missile which is effective in combats up to 60,000 ft (18300 m). Its Mk 2 version entered service in 1969 and was credited with the destruction of over 100 aircraft in the 1973 war. Seeking an improved version with longer range, the IDF/AF commissioned the Python 3, this seeing its operational debut against the Syrian air force in 1982, when it was claimed to have a better performance than the similar AIM-9L Sidewinder.

The same conflict probably saw the Luz 1 used in action for the first time, the weapon having been fitted to Kfirs and Phantoms from 1977 onwards. This is a

Despite its formidable cost, both to purchase and to operate, the McDonnell Douglas F-15 Eagle serves as a major type in today's IDF/AF. So far a total of 40 has been supplied, made up of F-15A and F-15C single-seaters, one of which is illustrated, and F-15B two-seaters.

McDonnell Douglas
F-15A Eagle

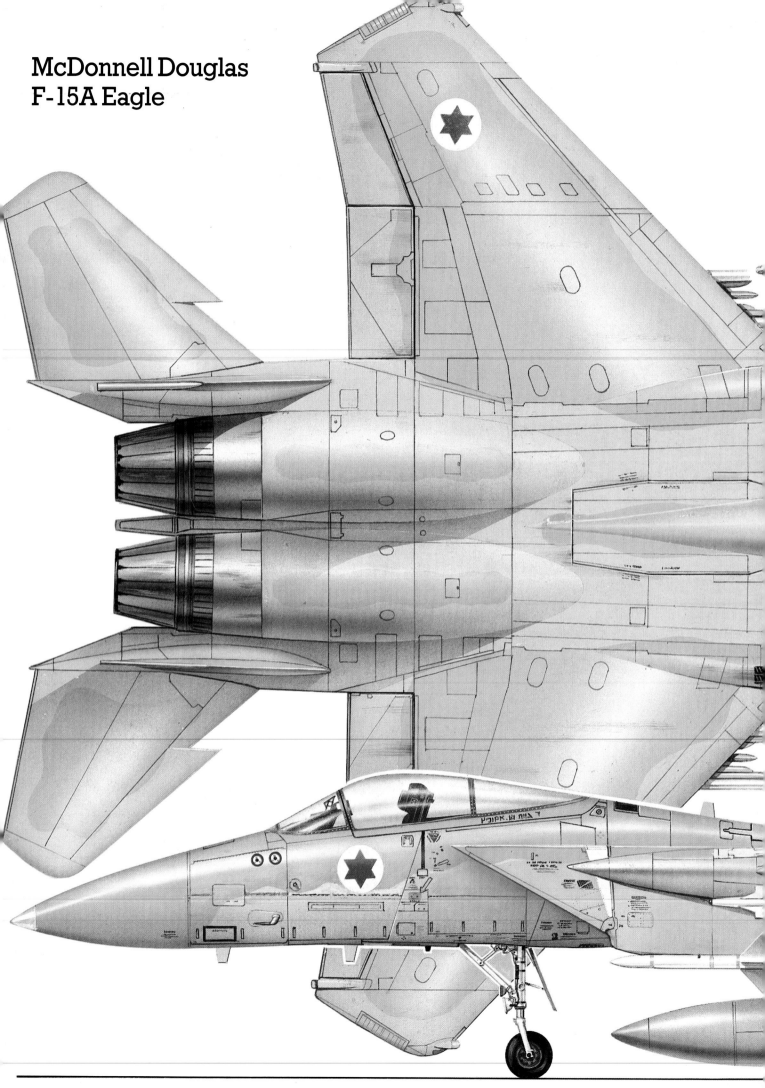

This F-15 Eagle is believed to be an F-15A version, though security is tight and little can be deduced from the often-changed (or, it seems, deliberately misleading) service number painted on all IDF/AF aircraft. Most Israeli F-15s carry the tail badge of an eagle on a red ace of spades, though this may not denote membership of any particular combat unit. The AIM-9J type Sidewinders are unusual.

McDonnell Douglas F-15A Eagle

This Israeli Eagle was one of the original batch of F-15As supplied from December 1976, though its apparent Sidewinder AIM-9B missiles would really have been AIM-9L type, supplied a short time later. The really important acquisition was the AIM-7 Sparrow in its long-range AIM-7F version, later the AIM-7M also being added. Allied with the APG-63 radar, these give the Eagle a great stand-off kill capability.

Specification

McDonnell Douglas F-15A Eagle

Type: single-seat air-superiority fighter

Powerplant: two Pratt & Whitney F100-PW-100 afterburning turbofans each of about 25,000-lb (111340-kg) static thrust

Performance: maximum speed (time limited) 1,650 mph (2655 km/h) or Mach 2.5 at altitude, or 936 mph (1506 km/h) or Mach 1.23 at sea level; service ceiling 63,000 ft (19200 m); radius of action about 600 miles (966 km)

Weights: empty 27,000 lb (12247 kg); normal take-off, clean, with four AIM-7 Sparrow missiles 41,500 lb (18824 kg); maximum take-off 56,000 lb (25402 kg)

Dimensions: span 42 ft 9½ in (13.04 m); length 63 ft 9½ in (19.44 m); height 18 ft 6 in (5.64 m); wing area 608 sq ft (56.48 m^2)

Armament: one 20-mm M61A1 cannon with 940 rounds, four AIM-7F Sparrow and four AIM-9L Sidewinder Shafrir 2 or Python 3 air-to-air missiles and five external store locations for a maximum of 16,000 lb (7258 kg) of disposable stores

A perfect plan view of an Israeli F-15 in full afterburner. Thanks to the use of the Grumman E-2C Hawkeye, these costly aircraft have not been placed in hazardous positions, yet have been able to sweep local areas clear of hostile aircraft.

TV-guided ASM which is intended primarily for attacks against SAM sites, although the IDF/AF has stated that the principal weapon used against Syrian missile installations was the conventional 'iron' bomb, backed up by the US-built Maverick missile. (The IDF/AF says its Mavericks are so accurate that it is considering using them without an explosive warhead, leaving the missile's kinetic energy to do the damage.)

Eagles over Israel

Whilst the Kfir is an all-purpose fighter, specialized air defence duties are assigned to a US-built combat aircraft, the F-15 Eagle. Most advanced of the USAF's interceptors, the Eagle was allocated to the IDF/AF as part of a move by the USA to limit Israel's offensive capabilities.

Originally, Israel had asked for a number of Pershing SSMs (without their normal nuclear warheads) but when the ability to produce nuclear weapons was claimed in 1974, the USA shied away from providing a delivery system. The CIA subsequently verified the Israeli holding as some 200 warheads, some of which are fitted in 40 Dassault MD.660 Jericho SSMs, which have a range of 280 miles (450 km). An alternative defensive package was offered (and accepted), including 23 F-15As, two F-15B trainers and four Grumman E-2C Hawkeyes.

Eagles were delivered to No. 133 Squadron from December 1976 onwards, armed with AIM-7F Sparrows and AIM-9L Sidewinders, a further 15 arriving during 1981-2 as a result of the Camp David agreement. Provision was made for the IDF/AF to order a further 15, but when the contract was placed in 1982, it covered only 11 because of funding problems. These aircraft will be armed with the latest AIM-7M Sparrows following a 1983 order for 150, Israel being the first country outside the USA to receive the air-launched version of the AIM-7M.

The Eagle participated in its first offensive operation in March 1978, uneventfully providing top cover for a strike against Palestine Liberation Organization bases in Lebanon, but first blood was drawn on 27 June 1979, when five Syrian Mikoyan-Gurevich MiG-21s were shared with Kfirs during an overflight of Lebanon. This was the first air combat between the IDF/AF and an Arab country since the Yom Kippur War six years earlier, such events becoming increasingly regular as Israel made repeated raids on PLO camps in retaliation for terrorist attacks.

An unconfirmed report suggests that the Eagle may have claimed its first MiG-23 'Flogger' on 13 February 1981, but it is almost certain that the two Syrian MiG-23s shot down over Lebanon on 21 April 1982 were the first of the type lost in combat, quite probably to Eagles. By the end of the 1982 incursion into Lebanon, the F-15 had increased its air fighting score to 58 without loss, mostly obtained by Sidewinders.

An important factor in the Eagle's success (and, indeed, in the whole Israeli command and control network) has been the Hawkeye, four of which have been in operation since December 1977. Though produced in the US for carrier operation by the navy, the Hawkeye has a remarkable overland capability and can even detect the movement of vehicles with its AN/AP S-125 radar and associated radar-processing system. The principal requirement is for location of aircraft, in which role the Hawkeye can track 250 targets while directing over 30 interceptions by friendly fighters. First used operationally in June 1979 (directing the Eagle/Kfir combat described above), the aptly-named Hawkeye has proved to be a vital asset in IAF hands.

Agile Fighting Falcon

Almost from the moment of the prototype's first flight, battle-hardened Israeli pilots were keen to get their

Taxiing, this F-15 shows the hinged engine inlets in the depressed configuration, matched to slow-speed flight at high AOA (angle of attack). It is not yet known how many F-15 combats have involved use of the gun, or Israeli AAMs.

General Dynamics F-16A Fighting Falcon

This General Dynamics F-16A Fighting Falcon was one of the first batch to be supplied to Israel, distinguished by its small horizontal tail. Three types of camouflage have been seen on Israeli F-16s, the others being a desert scheme (without green) and plain grey. This aircraft has a Falcon tail badge which, as in the case of the Eagles, may not be an actual badge of an IDF/AF squadron. The wingtip missiles shown here are AIM-9L Sidewinders.

248

Keith Fretwell.

General Dynamics F-16A Fighting Falcon

An IDF/AF F-16A, shown in the three-colour camouflage but without the Falcon badge on the fin. At the time of writing, all IDF/AF single-seat Falcons are of the original F-16A type, though it is possible that Israeli industry may have slightly augmented the mission avionics. The extended rear fuselage ECM (as used, for example, by Norway) has not been in evidence.

Specification
General Dynamics F-16A
Type: single-seat air combat fighter
Powerplant: one 23,830-lb (10807-kg) thrust Pratt & Whitney F100-PW-200 afterburning turbofan
Performance: maximum speed (clean) 1,320 mph (2112 km/h) or Mach 2.0; service ceiling 60,000+ ft (18290+ m); operating radius with six 500-lb (227-kg) Mk 82 bombs on hi-lo mission 685 miles (1102 km), or on lo-lo mission 340 miles (547 km); ferry range 2,215 miles (3565 km)
Weights: empty 15,137 lb (6865 kg); air superiority gross with two AIM-9 Sidewinders or Shafrirs 23,810 lb (10800 kg); maximum take-off 33,000 lb (14966 kg)
Dimensions: span with AIM-9 missiles 32 ft 10 in (10.01 m), without missiles 31 ft 0 in (9.45 m); length 47 ft $7^{7}/_{10}$ in (14.52 m); height 16 ft $5^{1}/_{5}$ in (5.01 m); wing area 300 sq ft (27.87 m^2)
Armament: one M61A-1 20-mm cannon with 500 rounds; nine external store stations carry up to 15,200 lb (6893 kg) of bombs, rockets, missiles, or other stores

hands on the agile F-16 Fighting Falcon. Ordered in quantity by the USAF and NATO (and later released to other customers), the Falcon is a nimble yet potent interceptor and strike aircraft ideally suited to air battles usually seen in Middle Eastern skies. In the interceptor role the F-16 is armed with Sidewinders and cannon for visual fighting, and in the strike role can carry a range of ordnance including laser-guided bombs.

The IDF/AF at first proposed to obtain 250 Falcons, comprising 50 built by General Dynamics in the US and the remainder as licensed production by IAI, but this was turned down. Instead, Washington authorized an initial batch of 67 F-16As and eight F-16B trainers, the first of which was handed over in January 1980 at Hill AFB, Utah, where IDF/AF pilots received their training. Even before the last of three units (one of these is known to be No. 117 Squadron) was equipped with the new aircraft, the Falcon had participated in its first daring raid.

Israel had long been concerned that its neighbours were on the road to producing their own nuclear weapons, and feared that the reactor being built at Tamux, about 15 miles (24 km) south east of the Iraqi capital, Baghdad, would shortly begin production of bomb material. Damage to the plant had been caused by two Phantoms on 30 September 1980 (they were originally thought to be Iranian, although Israel was probably responsible), but the IDF/AF planned to complete the job with Operation 'Babylon'.

After a six-month training period by selected units, eight Falcons, escorted by six Eagles, took off from Etzion air base in the Sinai Desert on 7 June 1981 at the start of a 1,120-mile (1800-km) round trip. This was accomplished without inflight-refuelling, and required the Eagles to refrain from use of afterburner at take-off to conserve fuel. Most Falcons carried a pair of 2,000-lb (907-kg) Mk 84 bombs, two 370-US gal (1400-litre) wing tanks and a 300-US gal (1136-litre) tank beneath the fuselage.

Flying over north west Saudi Arabia and skirting Jordan, the aircraft responded in Arabic when challenged by a Jordanian radar unit and timed their sortie to avoid detection by the USAF Boeing E-3A Sentries providing radar cover of Saudi territory.

Though Iraq air force units were supposedly on alert because of that country's war with Iran, the Falcons and Eagles had an uninterrupted flight, the former dropping their bombs with pinpoint accuracy in a single pass attack which left enough damage to set back the

A pre-delivery picture of an Israeli F-16, armed with AIM-9J Sidewinders. The undersides appear to be plain grey in all IDF/AF aircraft; surprisingly, radomes are not painted.

Of the original General Dynamics Fighting Falcon batch, eight were of the two-seat F-16B variety, one of which is seen here in the 'desert' style camouflage. These aircraft were used to train the first pilots at Hill AFB in the USA.

This F-16A, no. 135, probably carries the Fighting Falcon tail badge, because close inspection of the original shows that this area has been retouched by a censor. AIM-9J Sidewinders are fitted.

reactor programme by between three and five years. Thanks to their extensive ECM (electronic countermeasures) equipment, the worst which the IDF/AF aircraft had to encounter was undirected AA fire, and all arrived safely back at base.

This first combat mission by an F-16 anywhere in the world caused the US acute embarrassment, and as diplomatic protests flew back and forth, the USA withheld deliveries of the 22 Falcons remaining to be delivered and the second batch of 15 Eagles. Two months later, however, the supply was resumed.

By May 1982, the IDF/AF had been permitted to order a second batch of Falcons, but the very next month its invasion of Lebanon again halted US arms contracts. Only after almost a year, when Israel agreed to withdraw its occupation forces, was the order allowed to proceed, with delivery of the first aircraft accordingly delayed by the same interval to December 1986. The batch will comprise F-16Cs and probably a few F-16D trainers.

Having lost three Falcons in accidents, the IDF/AF

had 72 available for its 1982 adventure in Lebanon, and the curtain was raised on 4 June when seven waves of aircraft struck at Palestinian camps on the outskirts of Beirut. Reports of the action are confused, some claiming only the involvement of Falcons, others that Phantoms and Skyhawks were employed. The battle rapidly developed as the Israeli army marched north and the IDF/AF unleashed its fury at the SAM sites which Syria had installed in the Bekaa Valley.

By the well-planned use of decoy drones, jamming and E-2C Hawkeyes for airborne control, the IDF/AF caused the complete collapse of the Syrian air command structure, reducing the Syrians to launching mass attacks without direction. The result was predictable: Israel claimed to have shot down 85 aircraft in air-to-air combat (and destroyed another seven on the ground) for the loss of two fighters and a helicopter to ground fire. Of these, Falcons claimed 44 MiG-21 'Fishbeds' and MiG-23 'Floggers' at no loss to themselves and with 100 per cent aircraft serviceability each morning. Most combats took place in three hectic days (9-11 June) and involved Sidewinder and Shafrir AAMs (with the Python 3 probably making its service debut), but for various reasons, Israel later played down the role of the Falcon and Eagle. According to later statements, Kfirs (taking part in their first large operation) and Phantoms were the workhorses in Lebanon, although this appears to relate to ground-attack operations.

Phantom: still a valuable asset

Developed for carrierborne interceptor and strike roles during the mid-1950s, the Phantom now serves a dozen air forces as a land-based combat aircraft. The aircraft was widely used by the US Navy and US Air Force during the Vietnam War, and by the time it reached Israel the type had already proved itself to be one of the most outstanding aircraft of its day. As befits such a successful design, the Phantom enjoyed a long production run amounting to 5,201 aircraft, the last of which was delivered (from the second production line

in Japan) as recently as May 1981.

In all, the IDF/AF received 204 F-4E versions of the Phantoms, together with a further 12 reconnaissance RF-4Es. First deliveries took place in 1969 in the form of 44 aircraft ordered by the USAF in the previous fiscal year. These were followed by 18 from 1971 contracts and 24 from 1974 orders, while the RF-4Es came in two batches of six out of 1969 and 1975 contracts. In addition to these 98 factory-fresh Phantoms, a further 118 F-4Es were diverted from the USAF, a large number of them to replace losses in the Yom Kippur War. The first to arrive were taken from US squadrons based in Europe, but others came from the US and their speedy re-allocation was of immense value to the IDF/AF at a time when it was sorely pressed. By 1980, Israel had lost 56 of its 204 F-4Es from all causes.

The five squadrons now operating Phantoms (two of which are based at Hatzor) operate principally in the strike role, as indicated by the fact that despite its earlier successes, the aircraft made only one air-to-air claim during the Lebanon campaign in 1982. Phantoms have a considerable armoury including locally-built 30-mm DEFA cannon, McDonnell Douglas Harpoon anti-ship missiles, Hobos TV-guided stand-off bombs, Texas Instruments Shrike anti-radiation missiles, Hughes/Martin Walleye ASMs and Hughes Maverick ASMs.

In Lebanon, however, the Phantoms' principal weapon was the conventional bomb, backed up by the General Dynamics Standard ASM, with which they participated in the destruction of 19 SAM sites, including 10 in the first 10 minutes of the attack! The usual

The status of the IAI Nesher in Israeli service is unknown, many having been sold off to the Argentine forces (and used in the Falklands conflict). It is likely that some remain, possibly in use as weapons trainers.

Employed now in the attack role, the Israeli F-4E Phantoms have seen much action against the MiG-21s of the surrounding Arab nations, gaining the upper hand (largely due to the superior tactics of the pilots and the weapon systems of the Phantom) during the 1973 Yom Kippur war. The F-4E differed from earlier models by having a 20-mm Vulcan gun mounted under the nose for close-in air combat.

An Israeli F-4E with its inflight-
refuelling probe extended. Lockheed
KC-130 tanker support is occasionally
needed, though most F-4E missions
are tasked without it.

McDonnell Douglas F-4E Phantom II

This shark-mouth adornment was seen on some of the first F-4Es to reach Israel, and is distinctly unusual within the IDF/AF. From the start, on 7 January 1970, the Phantoms have been used mainly in the surface attack role, their capability being such that at times the inventory of available ordnance ran dangerously low.

Specification

McDonnell Douglas F-4E Phantom II

Type: two-seat multi-role fighter

Powerplant: two 17,900-lb (8119-kg) thrust General Electric J79-GE-17 afterburning turbojets

Performance: maximum speed (clean) 1,432 mph (2304 km/h) or Mach 2.17; initial climb (clean) 49,800 ft (15180 m) per minute; service ceiling 62,250 ft (18975 m); operating radius (four AIM-7F Sparrows, one Mk 28 and two tanks) hi-lo-hi 422 miles (680 km); ferry range 1,611 miles (2593 km)

Weights: empty 30,328 lb (13770 kg); maximum loaded 61,795 lb (28055 kg)

Dimensions: span 38 ft 4 in (11.68 m); length 63 ft 0 in (19.2 m); height 16 ft 5 in (5.00 m); wing area 530 sq ft (49.24 m²)

Armament: one M161A-1 20-mm gun with 639/640 rounds; four AIM-7E2 or -7F Sparrow III missiles recessed under fuselage; centreline pylon for any tactical store including 3,020-lb (1370-kg) M118 HE, nuclear, fire, cluster or other bombs, SUU-16/A or -23/A gun pods, spray tank, two target or air-to-ground rockets; four wing pylons for Shrike, Standard ARM, Walleye, HARM or other missiles (inner pylons only can carry twin Sidewinder or other missiles); wide variety of ECM pods and tanks

mode of assault on the sites was a low-level run-in using terrain masking, with chaff and flares as additional protection, while other aircraft (probably Boeing 707s) provided stand-off jamming and drones acted as decoys.

When tackling tanks, Phantoms, Kfirs and Skyhawks used 5-in (127-mm) Zuni and 2.75-in (70-mm) rockets, bombs and an undisclosed type of new missile which is programmed to dive down on the vehicle's thinner upper-surface armour. This missile is said to be highly effective against even the formidable T-72 tank of Soviet manufacture.

Another new missile in prospect for the Phantom was revealed to be undergoing flight-testing early in 1983. Previously a ship-to-ship weapon, the IAI Gabriel in its Mk III A/S version has been modified for aerial carriage and launching, for which it is fitted with revised wing surfaces of greater aerodynamic efficiency. Two sub-types are being tested, of which the later has a new solid-propellant motor, extending its range from 42 to 56 miles (68 to 90 km) after a high-altitude launch. Terminal guidance is provided by an X-band frequency-agile radar seeker. Although intended primarily for the Phantom, the Gabriel Mk III A/S may also be fitted to the Skyhawk, Kfir and IAI Sea Scan.

Trials have been conducted of a Phantom fitted with the locally-produced Elta M-2021 radar, while an indigenous inertial navigation system has been installed to provide increased accuracy in single-pass

attacks. It is reported that reconnaissance Phantoms have also been fitted with Israeli 'black boxes' to boost their intelligence-gathering capabilities. The dozen RF-4Es have been augmented by an unknown number of F-4Ps, which are F-4Es converted by General Dynamics to carry electronic reconnaissance equipment.

The details of such modifications are closely guarded, and when an RF-4E was brought down in the Bekaa Valley during 1982, a Soviet team (reportedly of 11 personnel) hastened to the scene. The IDF/AF had already decided to destroy the aircraft, and an air strike arrived at the very moment that the Soviets were pulling components from the wreckage. Regardless, the force went ahead with its mission.

Skyhawk version

Also from the McDonnell Douglas stable, the robust little A-4 Skyhawk is a long-standing campaigner with the IDF/AF, and four squadrons retain the type for the close-support role. Of some 320 single-seat A-4s and 28 TA-4 trainers delivered to Israel, the earliest mark was the standard US Navy A-4E, about 100 being transferred between 1969 and 1974, together with 13 A-4Ms. The IDF/AF ordered a specialized verison designated A-4H, this having several new features compared with the A-4F from which it was developed. Two 30-mm DEFA cannon were mounted in the nose, and a revised fin and rudder (later adopted on the A-4K and subsequent models) were accompanied by a braking para-

This F-4E has been engaged in the development trials of the Israeli (IAI) Gabriel IIIAS air-to-surface missile, the release of one being recorded here in a frame from cine film.

McDonnell Douglas A-4E Skyhawk

No modern combat aircraft have been more intensively in action than the Israeli A-4 Skyhawks, of which about one-third of the original force of 306 have been lost. This example is an ex-US Navy A-4E with round-topped fin, updated in Israel with the camel hump, but shown here with the original jetpipe.

Specification
McDonnell Douglas A-4F Skyhawk
Type: single-seat attack aircraft
Powerplant: one 9,300-lb (4218-kg) thrust Pratt & Whitney J52-P-8A turbojet
Performance: maximum speed (clean) 655 mph (1054 km/h), (with 4,000-lb/1814-kg bombload) 631 mph (1015 km/h); initial climb rate 8,000 ft (2440 m) per minute; tactical radius (4,000-lb/1814-kg bombload) 380 miles (612 km)
Weights: empty 10,100 lb (4581 kg); maximum take-off 27,420 lb (12437 kg)
Dimensions: span 27 ft 6 in (8.38 m); length (excluding probe) 40 ft 4 in (12.29 m); height 15 ft 0 in (4.57 m); wing area 260 sq ft (24.16 m²)
Armament: centreline pylons 3,500 lb (1588 kg), inboard wing pylons each 2,250 lb (1020 kg) and outer wing pylons each 1,000 lb (454 kg), for the carriage of several hundred variations of stores to maximum normal weight 9,920 lb (4500 kg); two 30-mm DEFA each with 150 rounds

Surprisingly, perhaps, the IDF/AF is fond of putting on a display of its combat aircraft complete with weapons. This is a McDonnell Douglas A-4H or -4N Skyhawk II, with square-topped fin (with unexplained 'pimple').

chute in the tail.

Having received 90 A-4Hs, Israel next contracted for at least 86 (and probably 117) A-4N aircraft based on the A-4H but with an Elliott head-up display and other improved avionics, later bringing its older aircraft up to this standard. Skyhawks suffered heavily in the Yom Kippur War, and 53 were lost, compared with 33 Phantoms and 11 Mirages/Neshers. As a measure to improve survivability, aircraft were fitted with an ungainly extension to the jetpipe, the theory being that a heat-seeking missile will demolish this extraneous ironmongery and leave the vital tail surfaces relatively undamaged.

Delivery of F-16 Falcons has allowed the IDF/AF to reduce its Skyhawk inventory and sales have already been made, officially via the USA, to Indonesia (in whose service they still retain the long jetpipe). About 95 remain operational, including 20 trainers, and a further 60 are held in storage. Argentina was reported to be interested in obtaining some of these surplus aircraft after the Falklands war, but no transfers have yet been made.

Probably a very recent photograph, this fine landing picture shows an Israeli Skyhawk with 'every mod con', including the fin-top pimple (probably ECM) and the extended jetpipe. Guns are 30-mm.

Hughes Model 500MD Defender

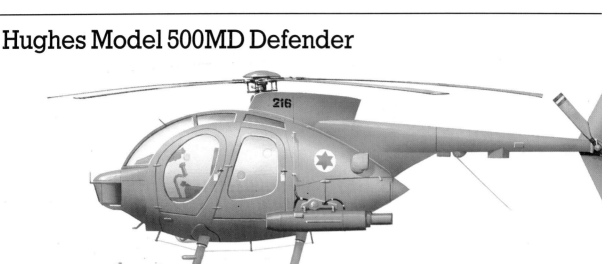

One of the newest types of combat aircraft in the IDF/AF, the Hughes Model 500MD is in service with every available bit of kit apart from the MMS (mast-mounted sight) which was not cleared for use when these helicopters were purchased. Particularly compact and agile, they have proved popular and capable, even in the hot Israeli environment which has laid low many otherwise famed aircraft.

Specification
Hughes 500MD Defender
Type: light multi-role military helicopter
Powerplant: one 420-shp (313-kW) Allison 250-C20B turboshaft
Performance: maximum cruising speed 160 mph (257 km/h) clean or 138 mph (222 km/h) with four TOW missiles; initial climb rate

1,650 ft (503 m) per minute; service ceiling 13,800 ft (4205 m); range with four TOWs 230 miles (370 km)
Weights: empty 1,320 lb (599 kg); maximum take-off 3,000 lb (1361 kg)
Dimensions: rotor diameter 26 ft 4 in (8.03 m); fuselage length 23 ft 0 in (7.01 m); height 8 ft 6 in (2.59 m); main rotor disc area 544.63 sq ft (50.60 m^2)
Armament: no permanent armament; options include four Hughes TOW anti-tank missiles, up to two 7.62-mm (0.3-in) General Electric M134 Miniguns or (later) Hughes EX-34 Chain Guns, four GD Stinger air-to-air missiles, one 40-mm grenade-launcher, and one seven-round unguided rocket pod.

Tank-killers

The air battles fought by the IDF/AF have been matched in their ferocity by action on the ground, where the spearhead is the tank. Israel has produced its own armoured fighting vehicles to augment those obtained from abroad, which are often modified, and these have been used to effect in conflicts since 1956. Arab nations opposing Israel are similarly armed (mostly with vehicles of Soviet manufacture), and thus the anti-tank helicopter has an important role to play on both sides.

Three squadrons of the IDF/AF are equipped with the Bell AH-1 Cobra which, although it looks very different to the UH-1 'Huey', is a close relative through use of common dynamic and airframe components. Israel uses three Cobra variants, including the initial

production model, the AH-1G, powered by a 1,100-shp (820-kW) Lycoming T53-13 and with various armament options such as two Miniguns or two 40-mm grenade-launchers (or one of each) in the nose turret, and four 19-round rocket packs or two 20-mm General Electric rotary cannon on the stub-wings.

By 1973, the AH-1Q TowCobra had evolved from the AH-1G, its name indicating fitment of a two-round launcher for the Hughes BGM-71 TOW anti-tank missile under each wing. Associated systems comprise a Sperry Rand (Univac) helmet sight system for both crew members, allowing them to use the TOW sight (with magnification power between ×2 and ×13) for the turret weapons as well as the missiles. About a dozen AH-1Gs and 18 AH-1Qs were supplied to the

A Hughes Model 500MD/TOW on parade on an IDF/AF open day, with a Bell 205 in the rear. Helicopters have always been of the greatest importance to the Israelis, and used in large numbers.

Bell AH-1S Cobra

Not only has the Bell AH-1 HueyCobra been supplied in different versions, but these have been modified in various ways after entering service in Israel. This is one of the latest AH-1S series, with uprated engine (with IR-suppressed jetpipe), TOW missiles and the M197 three-barrel 20-mm gun in the chin turret.

Specification
Bell Model 209 AH-1S
Type: anti-armour attack helicopter
Powerplant: one 1,800-shp (1343-ekW) Avco Lycoming T53-703 turboshaft
Performance: maximum speed varies from 270 mph (333 km/h) to 141 mph (227 km/h) depending on equipment fit; range at sea level with maximum fuel and eight per cent reserves 315 miles

(507 km)
Weights: empty 5,479 lb (2939 kg); maximum take-off 10,000 lb (4535 kg)
Dimensions: main rotor diameter 44 ft 0 in (13.41 m); fuselage length 44 ft 7 in (13.59 m); height over tail rotor 13 ft 6¼ in (4.12 m); main rotor disc area 1,520.5 sq ft (141.26 m²) or, in AH-1T, 1,809.6 sq ft (168.1 m²)
Armament: eight TOW missiles on outboard wing pylons, with pods inboard housing groups of seven or 19 of any of five types of 2.75-in (69.9-mm) rocket; General Electric turret under nose with M197 20-mm three-barrel gun (alternatives are 30-mm gun or combined 7.62-mm/0.3-in Minigun plus 40-mm grenade-launcher)

Probably originally built as a Bell AH-1G, this Cobra has been upgraded to AH-1Q standard with two quad TOW installations. The chin turret has a Minigun and a 40-mm grenade launcher.

IDF/AF, followed by an unknown number of the AH-1S variant.

The AH-1S is also TOW-equipped, but is a substantially improved model fitted with a 1,825-shp (1361-kW) T53-703 engine and upgraded dynamic components for better performance and manoeuvrability. Other changes from the earlier standard include a turreted cannon, improved fire-control and stores-management systems, flat glass panels (reducing glint and giving better protection against small-arms fire) and several modifications to improve technical reliability.

Complementing this force is the Hughes 500MD Defender, which is also TOW-armed but lacks the battlefield protection built into the Cobra. Deliveries totalled 32 during 1979, both types seeing action during the Lebanon invasion of 1982.

Hughes 500MD Defender

This Hughes Model 500MD/TOW is depicted in khaki-brown. A Defender has also been seen with the same number, 214, painted olive-green overall, but this could mean several things (there are cases of a number being seen on different aircraft, even of different types). This drawing shows the stabilized TOW sight in front of the gunner, who actually guides the missiles; it also provides a steering indication for the pilot.

Keith Fretwell

Grumman E-2C Hawkeye

Israel's four Grumman E-2C Hawkeye AEW platforms could well be considered the most important four aircraft in the country. Since their arrival in 1981 they have exceeded all expectations in acting as force-multipliers and reducing friendly losses. They have handled air situations over both land and water.

Specification
Grumman E-2C
Type: early warning and control aircraft
Accommodation: crew comprises pilot, co-pilot, CIC (combat information centre) officer, air control officer and radar operator

Powerplant: two 4,910-ehp (3663-ekW) Allison T56-A-425 turboprops
Performance: maximum speed 374 mph (602 km/h); range 1,605 miles (2583 km); endurance 6 hours 6 minutes
Weights: empty 37,945 lb (17211 kg); maximum take-off 51,817 lb (23503 kg)
Dimensions: span 80 ft 7 in (24.56 m); length 57 ft 6¾ in (17.54 m); height 18 ft 3¾ in (5.58 m); wing area 700.0 sq ft (65.03 m²)

Vital electronic warfare

Unarmed aircraft tend to attract less interest than their more lethal counterparts, and are often lumped together as second-line equipment with trainers and communications types. However, this misses the vital point that some are far more important to the IDF/AF than a whole squadron of fighter-bombers, for they both find the important targets to be struck and provide protection for the attacking aircraft from hostile fighters and SAMs.

The crucial role of the Grumman Hawkeye has already been discussed, although less easily-recognized aircraft undertake allied missions. The Boeing 707 is universlly known as a passenger transport, but five of those in IDF/AF service have a very different task to perform, being assigned to gathering electronic intelligence and generating jamming.

This is the twilight world of warfare, where secrets are even more closely guarded than normal, yet the basic function is clearly apparent. Electromagnetic waves (radio and radar) are indispensable to the functioning of individual weapons and whole defensive networks, and if they can be disrupted the attacker's position is strengthened manyfold.

First task is to identify the positions and frequencies of an opponent's equipment to provide target data for bombers or enable preparations to be made to jam systems which cannot be destroyed immediately. Cruising at height, the modified Boeings can gather this information from within Israeli airspace during peacetime, for all units need to train, and this entails the switching on of their equipment. Of course, potential opponents may not use the frequencies reserved for wartime, or may have the facility to change frequen-

One of the few available pictures showing an Israeli E-2C with a service number (these were not painted on until late 1982). For display purposes the rotodome has been raised to the flight position.

A low flypast by a Grumman E-2C, which spends its routine operating life at around 30,000 ft (9144 m). It is not known if Israel's Hawkeyes have the new TRAC-A antenna modification to improve radar performance.

Like Stratocruisers, Noratlases and many other types, the Israeli Grumman OV-1 Mohawks have carried civil registration as well as military insignia. They park with propellers feathered.

cies, so the electronic intelligence (Elint) aircraft must be ready to continue their work after the shooting starts.

Elint

Elint is a passive activity, in that the aircraft performing the duty stooges around silently listening. In support of combat operations during an offensive, other equipment is brought into active play to jam the opponent's transmissions. In its crudest form, jamming is simply the generation of a strong signal to obliterate the relevant one, or at least render it useless: for example, fighter control could be ruined by means no

more sophisticated than the production of a buzzing or screeching sound in the pilots' ears so that they are unable to understand instructions from the ground. It is almost certain that the IDF/AF uses more subtle means to confuse the enemy, such as an Arabic-speaking controller to issue false instructions, but this could be undertaken from a ground station in many cases.

In the successful attacks made on Syrian SAM sites in the Bekaa Valley, Boeing 707s provided stand-off jamming: distorting the signals from the ground-based radar associated with the missiles while the fighter-bombers made their deadly approach. The 'stand-off' is of some importance to the Boeing's crew, for an

Grumman OV-1B Mohawk

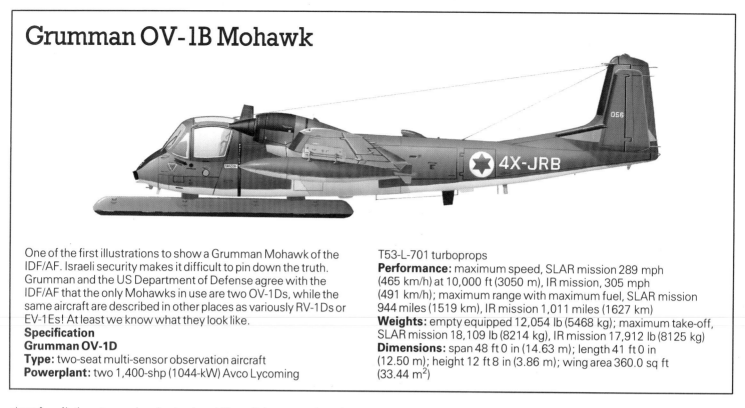

One of the first illustrations to show a Grumman Mohawk of the IDF/AF. Israeli security makes it difficult to pin down the truth. Grumman and the US Department of Defense agree with the IDF/AF that the only Mohawks in use are two OV-1Ds, while the same aircraft are described in other places as variously RV-1Ds or EV-1Es! At least we know what they look like.

Specification
Grumman OV-1D
Type: two-seat multi-sensor observation aircraft
Powerplant: two 1,400-shp (1044-kW) Avco Lycoming

T53-L-701 turboprops
Performance: maximum speed, SLAR mission 289 mph (465 km/h) at 10,000 ft (3050 m), IR mission, 305 mph (491 km/h); maximum range with maximum fuel, SLAR mission 944 miles (1519 km), IR mission 1,011 miles (1627 km)
Weights: empty equipped 12,054 lb (5468 kg); maximum take-off, SLAR mission 18,109 lb (8214 kg), IR mission 17,912 lb (8125 kg)
Dimensions: span 48 ft 0 in (14.63 m); length 41 ft 0 in (12.50 m); height 12 ft 8 in (3.86 m); wing area 360.0 sq ft (33.44 m^2)

aircraft radiating strong signals stands out like a lighthouse on a dark night and will attract fighters from hundreds of miles away.

The two main types of SAM encountered in Lebanon were the SA-2 (NATO reporting name 'Guideline') and the SA-6 ('Gainful'), both of them adversaries of old for the IDF/AF. SA-2s are supported by several radars (each with a NATO name) such as the 'Spoon Rest' for early warning, 'Fan Song' for tracking and 'Squint Eye' for acquisition. The IDF/AF has had their measure for some time, but a rude awakening came during the first few hours of the 1973 war when SA-6s hacked down Israeli aircraft at an alarming rate. The type proved unaffected by the jamming equipment then in use, and new apparatus (initially for use by strike aircraft) was rushed to the Middle East by the USA in a move to

combat the menace. Israel has now unlocked the secrets of the SA-6 and its 'Long Track' surveillance and 'Straight Flush' fire-control radars to such effect that Syria is believed to have fired over 300 SAMs during the Lebanon campaign and destroyed a mere three IDF/AF aircraft (and at least one of these fell to AA guns!). In this and earlier encounters, eye-witnesses have reported SAMs running amok after launch as a result of their radar guidance being jammed.

Sharing the Elint and jamming role are three types of aircraft used by the US Army, and thus presumably operated by the IDF/AF in support of its ground forces, although probably no clear-cut division of roles can be made. In mid-1976, two Grumman EV-1E Mohawks entered IDF/AF service, and these were followed in 1980 by a small number of Beech RU-21 military

Israel's Lockheed C-130s serve as air refuelling tankers as well as the standard heavy airlift transport. This example (a C-130E or C-130H) has unusual extra communications blade aerials above the flight deck.

Lockheed C-130H Hercules

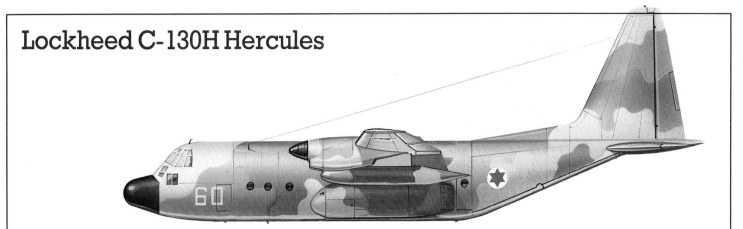

Probably one of the earlier Lockheed C-130s to join the IDF/AF, this example has no civil registration, normally seen on Israeli transports to facilitate passage through foreign countries. The C-130s usually have registrations beginning with letters FB. Camouflage patterns are non-standardized, being sprayed on haphazardly by hand . Note the two-figure code.

Specification
Lockheed C-130H Hercules
Type: military medium/long-range transport
Powerplant: four 4,508-shp (3362-kW) Allison T56-A-15 turboprops

Performance: maximum cruising speed 386 mph (621 km/h); range with maximum payload, 5% reserve and allowances for 30 minutes at sea level 2,487 miles (4002 km); range with maximum fuel, reserves and allowances as above 5,135 miles (8264 km)
Weights: operating (empty) 75,331 lb (34170 kg); maximum normal take-off 155,000 lb (70307 kg); maximum overload take-off 175,000 lb (79379 kg)
Dimensions: span 132 ft 7 in (40.41 m); length 97 ft 9 in (29.79 m); height 38 ft 3 in (11.66 m); wing area 1,745 sq ft (162.11 m²)

versions of the King Air. Further capability in this direction was obtained in 1983 on arrival of a few similar RC-12Ds. In US service these aircraft intercept and interrupt army communications and can also jam gun-laying radar.

Large transport force

The immensity of the IDF/AF's combat force is naturally dictated by the size of the air arms which oppose it, but for a small country with no overseas possessions or protectorates, Israel has an inordinately large transport element in its air force. With a few exceptions, the aircraft used in this role are tactical transports and heavy helicopters, their value being their ability to move troops (including paratroops) and equipment at high speed to any trouble spot. Such operations are not always within Israel's borders or the territory it occupies, as shown by the daring and effective commando assault on Entebbe Airport, Uganda, during 1976 to rescue hostages held by terrorists.

Such missions are rare, however, and the transport force normally goes about its mundane business of fetching and carrying out of the limelight. Providing the backbone of the transport element is the Lockheed Hercules, one of the world's best-known freighters. First flown in 1954 and still in production, the Hercules

serves with the IDF/AF in three marks, of which the first (but not the oldest) is the C-130H. Two of this variant were supplied late in 1971, followed by a further pair in 1974 (one of which crashed in 1975), and then Hercules were rapidly built up by the transfer of 12 C-130E models from the USAF. Total procurement of 24 was completed in 1976 with delivery of a further nine C-130H aircraft, including two KC-130H inflight-refuelling tankers.

Like most heavy transports, the Hercules are based at Ben Gurion Airport, Tel Aviv, and employ an unusual system of identity markings, combining military and civilian systems. All IDF/AF aircraft have a three-figure serial number which is apparently chosen at random but does not duplicate the marking applied to another aircraft, of any type, in current use. As an example of the diversity of this system, the 24 Hercules are numbered between 009 and 545. Aircraft which may be called on to visit foreign countries also wear civilian registrations of the normal type (4X- followed by three letters), although in this instance blocks of registrations are used and there is no effort made to scramble the markings to confuse observers.

Civilian registrations are usually worn only for flights outside Israel, but conversely, when an aircraft goes abroad, its squadron badge is normally painted over.

Flown on 7 March 1972, the prototype of the IAI 201, military version of the Arava, was not automatically bought by the IDF/AF but had to prove its worth. The ambulance was a gift from the American people.

The Israeli Air Force

The IDF/AF is particularly security-conscious, as will be seen from official photographs of aircraft on which the badge, and often serial number, has been erased by the censor. All that is known about the Hercules force is that two different badges have been observed on certain aircraft, implying two operating units.

A similar position obtains for the force of 13 Boeing 707s, all of which are former civilian transports. Again operated from Ben Gurion, five of these are equipped with inflight-refuelling equipment and others (as mentioned above) are used for electronic intelligence-gathering in a configuration approximating to the USAF's EC-135U. A few of the Boeings are operated on behalf of the Israeli government by Bedek Aircraft.

Medium transports comprise the IAI Arava and, inevitably, the veteran Douglas DC-3/C-47 Dakota. Reports speak of a dozen or so Aravas in service, including two in the electronic intelligence role, but there is little firm evidence to support this view and independent confirmation is available for only two aircraft. The ungainly twin-boom transport with its rotund fuselage has been exported around the world to the tune of some 130 examples and has obviously been a successful venture for the local aircraft industry.

Elint Aravas operated by the IDF/AF are equipped with a palletized installation which may also be fitted inside other transport aircraft, such as the Hercules. The unit comprises twin consoles for up to four operators and its prime component is the Elta L-8310 radar pulse-detection and measuring unit which is tied in with communications equipment (EK/K-7010) and several noise jammers (EL/L-8200 series) via an L-8312 computer.

No doubt surrounds the status of the 'Dak', of which about 15 are still operated from Ben Gurion on a variety of tasks. Dakotas have been a feature of the IDF/AF since its earliest days, and those presently in use have come from a variety of sources, including South Africa, the French air force, and civilian operators. It seems likely that they will remain for many more years to come.

Rotary-wing transports play an important role in supporting the Israeli army, and in this field the principal type is the Sikorsky S-65C-3 (CH-53D) Stallion, 33 of which have been supplied by the US manufacturer, complete with inflight-refuelling probes. Obviously well pleased with the capabilities of this powerful heavyweight, the IDF/AF obtained a further two S-65C-2s from the Austrian air force in 1981.

In the same role, the Sud (later Aérospatiale) SA 321K Super Frelon dates back to the days of military contacts with France. From 1965 onwards, 14 were built to IDF/AF order, although two crashed before they could be delivered. The survivors have had their three Turboméca Turmo engines replaced by General Electric T58s in order to improve performance and simplify maintenance requirements, as these turboshafts also power the CH-53.

Sikorsky CH-53D Stallion

Most powerful of Israeli helicopters, the Sikorsky S-65C-3 was supplied via the US Marine Corps, the machines being included in a regular USMC batch and transferred without announcement at the time. All IDF/AF S-65s have the 3,925 hp (2927-kW) T64-413 engine, fed through large inlet sand filters. Equipment includes armour, long-range drop tanks and flight-refuelling probes.

Specification

Sikorsky S-65C

Type: heavy transport and assault helicopter

Powerplant: two 3,925-shp (2927-kW) General Electric T64-413 turboshafts

Performance: maximum level speed at sea level 196 mph (315 km/h); cruising speed 173 mph (278 km/h); maximum rate of climb at sea level 2,180 ft (664 m) per minute; service ceiling 21,000 ft (6400 m); hovering ceiling in ground effect 11,700 ft (3565 m); hovering ceiling out of ground effect 4,300 ft (1310 m); range with two 450-US gal (1703-litre) auxiliary tanks and 10 per cent reserves 540 miles (669 km)

Weights: empty 23,569 lb (10690 kg); mission take-off 38,238 lb (17344 kg); maximum take-off 42,000 lb (19050 kg)

Dimensions: main rotor diameter 72 ft 3 in (22.02 m); tail rotor diameter 16 ft 0 in (4.88 m); fuselage length, excluding probe 67 ft 2 in (20.47 m); height overall 24 ft 11 in (7.60 m); main rotor disc area 4,070 sq ft (378.10 m^2)

The tail of this Aérospatiale Super Frelon bears the stencilling 'SA 321K no. 114'. As only 99 of all versions were made, this may mean that Israeli numbering ran from 101 to 114. This is one of the amphibious examples, with gear extended.

Communications and training

Light transport and communications work within the IDF/AF is assigned to several squadrons of aeroplanes and helicopters, the former category including 14 Do 28Bs, 20 or so Do 27s, 25 Cessna U206s and a few assorted Cessna 172s, 180s and 185s, many of which are based at Sde Dov, near Tel Aviv. Helicopters are more closely associated with the army, acting in the scouting and liaison roles, and some four squadrons operate 35 Bell 206s (including OH-58A Kiowas) and a similar

number of Bell 205s. Some of the last-mentioned are probably UH-1D Iroquois helicopters transferred from the US Army, but it is known that 13 Agusta (Bell) 205As were transferred to Rhodesia (now Zimbabwe) in 1978, while a few early Bell 205s have been sold on the civilian market, apparently after replacement by Bell 212s.

Aircrew training, based largely at Hatzerim, begins for pilots on the Piper Super Cub, some 20 remaining from at least 55 originally delivered. After this primary

Sprayed dull olive drab all over, this Sikorsky S-65 differs in some respects from most IDF/AF examples, and may be ex-Austrian. The service number on the nose is 652, but as this was on public view the number may be fictitious.

Beech and the IDF/AF insist that no ex-US Army RU-21s were ever supplied, and that Israeli Queen Airs are without exception regular commercially bought Beech B80s, used for multi-engine training and liaison.

A handful of Piper PA-18-150 Super Cubs are still used for initial grading of pupil pilots. Dozens of earlier Cubs have served the IDF/AF since 1948, some early ones as bombers!

Thanks to abundant engine power, (two at 290 hp/216 kW for only 6,000-lb/2722-kg gross weight), the Dornier Do 28B-1 has coped well in Israel in challenging transport, patrol and utility missions.

The Israeli Air Force

stage, basic instruction follows on the Fouga (Aéro-spatiale) CM.170 Magister, Bedek Aircraft having built this type under licence to augment other deliveries, including several from West Germany. In order to maintain the remaining 80 or so Magisters in operation well into the 1990s, IAI is rebuilding the fleet with improved avionics and uprated Marboré 6 engines, the finished product being known as the AMIT (Advanced Multi-mission Improved Trainer). A few Magisters have recently been obtained from abroad for AMIT conversion, and in this connection the disappearance of at least nine from Belgian air force surplus during 1980 may be relevant.

After their Magister/AMIT courses, which include weapons training on armed versions of the aircraft, future combat pilots undertake type conversion to front-line equipment, while transport personnel receive twin-engine training with the Flying School's fleet of some 20 Beech 80 Queen Airs.

Some of the pilots now receiving training are destined to fly a new combat aircraft which is presently taking shape on the drawing boards at IAI. Destined to replace the Skyhawk and later the Kfir, the Lavi will be an agile strike-fighter capable of carrying a typical load of eight 750-lb (340-kg) bombs over a combat radius of 275 miles (445 km) and mounting two Side-winder (or similar) AAMs for defensive or offensive operations. Thrust-to-weight ratio will be 1.1-to-1, indicating a performance comparable with the most advanced aircraft of its class anywhere in the world, including a speed of Mach 1.85.

Despite Israel's strong desire to become entirely self-sufficient in military equipment manufacture, the Lavi will be far from a 'home-grown' product. The advanced technology required to design, build and equip a combat machine of this sophistication is far beyond Israeli resources, and so large parts of the aircraft will be bought in from the US. Powered by a single Pratt & Whitney P1120 augmented turbojet of 20,620-lb (9353-kg) thrust and built under licence by Beit Shemesh, the Lavi will be borne aloft on carbon-fibre wings (and tail surfaces) furnished by Grumman, while a host of other American firms are to provide

components as diverse as brakes and electrical power systems.

By obtaining systems and whole structures previously perfected for US programmes, IAI hopes to keep the cost of the Lavi within Israel's limited means and at the same time acquire US technology and manufacturing expertise. Disadvantages, already becoming apparent, are that the US government will have control over the speed at which the design progresses and (as with the Kfir) a veto on overseas sales. The first of five prototypes (three of which will be two-seat trainers) is scheduled to fly early in 1986, and deliveries of 300 to the IDF/AF will begin in 1990.

Future plans

The Lavi is but the central element of a far-reaching improvement plan for the IDF/AF to increase in size

Almost unbelievably, there are no plans for any early retirement of the motley collection of IDF/AF Douglas C-47s and related 'DC-3' aircraft. A nominal total of 18 remain, some having been in Israel 25 years and possibly over 30.

Once fitted with bright red spinners, this Beech Queen Air B80 is now flying without them, though in other respects it remains immaculate. One of many duties is quick transport of local commanders to battle stations in emergency.

The Dornier Do 28B-1 was an improved model with modified wingtips serving as integral fuel tanks, and with an enlarged tailplane. This example has prominent extra radio blade aerials.

Numerically the versatile Bell Huey has always been the no. 1 Israeli helicopter. Early deliveries were all Bell-built, but they were later augmented by Agusta-built AB.205s, some being passed on to Zimbabwe. This is a later twin-engined Model 212 (UH-1N standard).

The twin-flamingo badge seen on IDF/AF Fouga Magisters may be that of the pilot training school at Hatzerim, though it is worn by Magisters only. This example is one of the rebuilt AMIT (advanced multi-mission improved trainer) type.

Bell Model 212

Because of their intensive utilization all over Israel it is hard to believe the IDF/AF bought only 12 Bell 212 helicopters (in fact this announced figure is believed now to be half the true one). Powered by the PT6T coupled turbine engine with two power sections of 1,025-hp (764-kW) each, the 212 (Twin Two-Twelve) has much better flight performance than older Hueys in hot and high conditions. They have very complete avionics, and rescue hoists.

Specification
Bell Model 212
Type: utility and light assault helicopter
Powerplant: one Pratt & Whitney of Canada PT6T-3B Twin Pac, comprising two PT6 turboshaft engines coupled to a single shaft producing 1,342 KW (1,800 hp), flat-rated to 962 kW (1,290 shp) for take-off

Performance: maximum speed (at maximum take-off weight) 161 mph (259 km/h); maximum range with standard fuel at sea level 261 miles (420 km)

Weights: empty 6,143 lb (2,787 kg); maximum take-off 11,200 lb (5,080 kg)

Dimensions: main rotor diameter 48 ft 2¼ in (14.69 m); fuselage length 42 ft 4¾ in (12.92 m); height over tail rotor 14 ft 10¼ in (4.53 m); main rotor disc area 1871.91 sq ft (173.9 m²)

from its present 580 combat aircraft to an interim 705 in 1987, before levelling out at about 600 during the 1990s as the Phantom, Kfir and Skyhawk (currently constituting 81 per cent of strength) become outmoded and are withdrawn. Only one Skyhawk squadron will remain in the training role by 1995, compared with the 175 aircraft now in service, while Phantom numbers will drop from 132 now to 100 in 1991 before falling even more rapidly. Production of 18 Kfirs per year up to 1986 will result in 220 of the type in use at that time, but this will reduce to 100 by 1995.

With Skyhawk and Kfir replacement taken care of by the Lavi, the IDF/AF is now looking at a follow-on for the Phantom, its present thinking being in favour of a two-type solution of F-16E Falcons and Northrop's land-based F-18L version of the McDonnell Douglas

This Bell 206 JetRanger is olive drab overall, most in IDF/AF service being camouflaged in three colours. All have very comprehensive avionics, and some have unexplained installations along the belly.

This IDF/AF Bell 212 has the type's usual long wire aerial, probably for HF communications, along the underside of the rear fuselage. The 212s are used for anything from VIP taxi to front-line resupply.

Popularly called Cessna Skywagons in the IDF/AF, the U206 Stationair serves in substantial numbers as a multi-role maid of all work. This one has six seats and a ventral cargo pack.

Almost all the Dornier Do 27Q STOL multi-role aircraft bought in 1964 are still flying. They have extra-large tyres and a typically comprehensive suite of avionics.

F/A-18A Hornet. If procurement of these types can be arranged, they will equip some of the planned 24 combat squadrons based at 10 airfields during the late 1990s.

Sadly, according to the law of averages, Israel will have had at least one more major conflict with its Arab neighbours before the current IDF/AF modernization plan has been completed. The odds have shifted considerably in Israel's favour since the IDF/AF was first called to battle, both Egypt and Jordan having turned to diplomacy to resolve their differences with the Jewish state, but war with Syria could still inflict serious damage on Israel. Local politics, shaped in response to the global strategies of the superpowers and influenced by the regional leader, Saudi Arabia, will control the course of events in the Middle East, yet amongst all these imponderables one fact is beyond doubt: if again brought into action, the Heyl Ha'Avir (Hebrew name for Israel's air force) may be relied upon to fight with the same professionalism and effectiveness which it has displayed in every one of its previous battles.

The Israeli Navy

The geographical position of Israel prevents its navy from playing a major part in a Middle East conflict, but it has an important role in keeping the coastlines of Israel free of attacks and access to the ports open. In numerical terms the navy is small, but it packs a powerful punch. Most of the ships are little more than patrol boats, but modern technology has endowed them with an ability to destroy enemy ships many times their size with guided anti-ship missiles such as the home-produced Gabriel. Coupled to this powerful weaponry the Israeli navy displays a powerful attacking spirit that has frequently provided it with a winning advantage, and its small size has nonetheless prevented their numerically more powerful foes from ruling the seas near Israel's coastlines.

Left: One of the two 'Dvora' class missile boats at speed. They are ideal for operations off Lebanon, screening amphibious forces against possible missile attack from Syrian naval units and releasing the larger missile craft for offensive roles.

Below: A 'Reshef' class vessel is used to test the IAI Barak short-range point defence SAM system. This is gradually taking the place of the SA-7 'Grail' and Redeye IR-guided shoulder-launched missiles currently used.

Where hard economics and politics decide the size of a nation's fleet, its shape will be moulded by a combination of geography and the form of the likely opposition.

Israel's shores comprise some 155 miles (250 km) of Mediterranean coast, with shallow approaches, and a narrow frontage onto the Gulf of Aqaba in the south. Politically, this latter sea access is highly desirable as it conveniently bypasses the Suez Canal for traffic to the east. In naval terms, this second piece of coast is a headache, for although only 620 miles (1000 km) distant from the Mediterranean littoral by sea with the canal open, maritime communication with this 'second front' in the event of a canal closure involves a voyage around the whole African continent. Effectively, therefore,

dispositions need to be made before the outbreak of hostilities. As maritime connections between one and the other are so difficult in wartime, the Israelis have set up base facilities at Eilat on the Gulf of Aqaba in addition to those at Ashod and Haifa, at each end of their Levant coast.

Opposition, in varying degrees of hostility, stems from the bulk of the Arab world. In practical naval terms it can be exercised only by neighbouring littoral states, namely Syria, Lebanon and Egypt. Of these, Egypt is potentially the most powerful but has been party to a controversial rapprochement that, for the time being at least, has reduced the prospect of further conflict. Lebanon is kept in a state of permanent disarray and represents no credible threat. Syria, on the

The Israeli navy operates two 'Dvora' class missile boats that were constructed by Israel Aircraft Industries to a private design. The 'Dvora' class is essentially an improvement of the 'Dabur' class, fitted with two missiles.

other hand, is well armed with Soviet-supplied warships and, although reported to be looking West for further sources, could rely on rapid replacement from the Soviets (if it suited them) in time of war or, failing this, the ubiquitous Libyans. Though no Arab state has a recent maritime tradition, or the necessary infrastructure to create and maintain a fleet, this is an age where technology is available for instant delivery on easy terms.

Like that of the then-hostile Egyptians, the Israeli fleet of the 1960s was a ragbag of 'hand-me-downs', largely of British origin. When their destroyer *Eilat* was shattered on Trafalgar Day 1967 by a pair of 'Styx' SSMs launched by Egyptian 'Osa' class attack craft from within the safety of their own harbour, the Israelis were as shaken as the remainder of the Western maritime world. The big gun had been eclipsed by the missile and this fact could no longer be ignored.

Like others before them (the Swedes, Danes, Norwegians and West Germans), the Israelis concluded that even to exist in narrow seas dominated by enemy aircraft and electronics, they would need to retire larger conventional warships in favour of small, fast and agile craft.

The Soviets had led the way through their introduction of the fast attack craft (FAC), in wedding hitting power with compactness; some maritime powers concentrated on the development of suitable antidotes, while others (including Israel) followed a similar path.

In the basic TNC 45 design from the experienced West German firm Lürssen they saw a suitable vessel,

19.7 ft (6 m) longer than the 128-ft (39-m) Soviet-built 'Osa' class craft and far more weatherly. Political considerations precluded the construction of such craft in West Germany, so the dozen required were ordered in two sets of six from CMN at Cherbourg, being delivered in 1968-9. All have steel hulls and light alloy upperworks, the first group ('Saar 2') being supplied with an all-40 mm gun armament and the second ('Saar 3') a 3-in (76-mm) weapon forward.

Interchangeability

Ease of weapon interchangeability is, however, a feature of Lürssen designs and all were soon fitted with the home-produced Gabriel Mk I SSM in a variety of mixes, using single and triple mountings. This type of missile carried a 143-lb (65-kg) warhead out to about 12.4 miles (20 km) but, while large enough to disable a small warship, it was too small for autonomous homing. Being semi-active, it required the launching ship to illuminate the target, limiting the rate at which missiles could be launched and exposing the ship to countermeasures. While up to eight Gabriels could be carried as a result of their small size, their range was only half that of the SS-N-2 'Styx' aboard the 'Osa' class craft.

Improved versions of the Gabriel have been developed in the Mks II and III, while the problem of range was solved in 1978 with the purchase of the Harpoon. Currently, 'Saar 3' craft are usually armed with a mix of Gabriel Mk IIs and a pair of Harpoons, while the 'Saar 2' craft have tended to trade a heavy Gabriel fit for a small sonar and ASW torpedoes. Of the

Although used by the Israeli navy, the 'Dvora' class were built for the export market, with Taiwan having licence-built over 35 units to a slightly modified design as the 'Hai Ou' class. The 'Dvora' are the smallest missile craft yet built in the world, and are equipped to carry two Gabriel anti-ship missiles using the Elta EL/M-2221 I/J band radar for control. It is probable that the new Gabriel Mk III active radar-homing missile will also be carried, as the fire control radar already has built-in facilities to handle it.

The air-launched Gabriel Mk III was developed from the active radar ship launched version to give the Israeli air force a potent anti-ship capability for its strike aircraft. Argentina is also thought to have bought it for its McDonnell Douglas A-4 Skyhawk units.

Arab states, only Egypt and Libya currently operate submarines and the ASW-equipped craft are, in any case, concentrated on Eilat, whose approaches are deeper than those of the Mediterranean ports.

Though all 12 of the early boats were high powered, with a 3,500-bhp (2610-kW) diesel on each of four shafts to develop a speed of 40 kts, the need to outperform an 'Osa' craft is not so evident on the later 'Saar 4' craft. This group of 10 have 188.6-ft (57.5-m) hulls to another Lürssen design, yet have installed power of some 25 per cent less. Though basically the same craft as that

operated by the Bundesmarine as the Type 143, the 'Saar 4' craft (often known as 'Reshef' craft after the lead unit) were built at Haifa, emphasizing the increasing independence of Israel from sensitive foreign governments.

Despite first being introduced more than 10 years ago the 'Saar 4' type is still being built. Voyages across the Atlantic and around the African continent impressed other fleets in need of performance craft. Chile has purchased a couple (and is reportedly interested in three more) to pursue her interests in the

'Dvora' class fast missile craft

Specification
Displacement: 47 tons full load
Dimensions: length 64.9 ft (19.8 m); beam 18 ft (5.5 m); draught 2.6 ft (0.8 m)
Propulsion: two diesels delivering 5,440 shp (4057 kW) to two shafts
Speed: 36 kts
Complement: 8-10
Armament: two single Gabriel Mk I/II SSM launchers, two single 20-mm and two single 12.7-mm (0.5-in) machine-guns
Electronics: one Elta EL/M-2221 fire control radar; one Decca 926 navigation radar

Israel Aircraft Industries Gabriel anti-ship missile

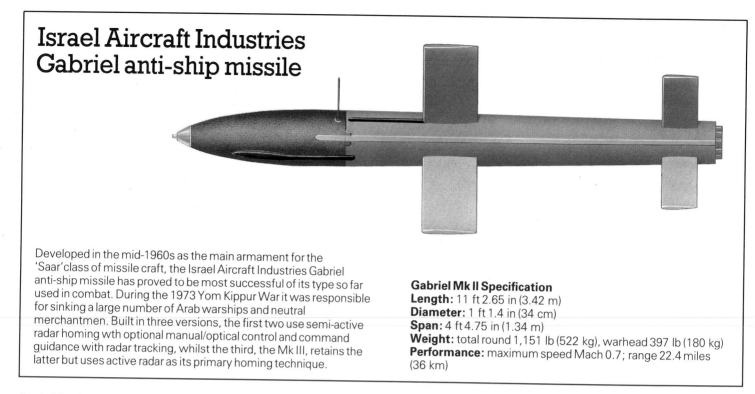

Developed in the mid-1960s as the main armament for the 'Saar' class of missile craft, the Israel Aircraft Industries Gabriel anti-ship missile has proved to be most successful of its type so far used in combat. During the 1973 Yom Kippur War it was responsible for sinking a large number of Arab warships and neutral merchantmen. Built in three versions, the first two use semi-active radar homing wth optional manual/optical control and command guidance with radar tracking, whilst the third, the Mk III, retains the latter but uses active radar as its primary homing technique.

Gabriel Mk II Specification
Length: 11 ft 2.65 in (3.42 m)
Diameter: 1 ft 1.4 in (34 cm)
Span: 4 ft 4.75 in (1.34 m)
Weight: total round 1,151 lb (522 kg), warhead 397 lb (180 kg)
Performance: maximum speed Mach 0.7; range 22.4 miles (36 km)

South Atlantic winter against a neighbouring Argentina intent on acquiring more soil. Three more have been built at Haifa for South Africa, with at least six more to follow from an indigenous yard at Durban. Like the Israelis, the South Africans have been thrown greatly on their own resources as traditional sources of armaments ran dry. The rapidly developing Israeli defence electronics industry has aided the South Africans also in the Skorpioen SSMs with which the South African craft are fitted, these missiles being closely similar to, if not identical with, the Gabriel Mk II. The choice of the 'Saar 4' type at all would seem a trifle strange as South Africa is bounded by the deep and turbulent southern ocean, for which more orthodox displacement warships would perhaps be better suited.

All operational 'Saar 4' craft carry Harpoon, being armed with as many as eight of these missiles. To realize their full over-the-horizon range of 62 miles (100 km), however, some form of mid-course correction is usually required. Experimentally, a Bell Kiowa helicopter was operated from a temporary pad on *Tarshish* to assess its potential not only as an aerial data link but also as a means of seducing incoming SSMs. In the latter mode, a helicopter can prove very attractive to a seeker of limited intelligence, luring the missile from its intended target and then losing it by superior agility.

The *Tarshish* trials resulted in the six-vessel 'Alia' class, basically 'Saar 4' craft with hulls stretched to nearly 203 ft (62 m) to accommodate both flight pad

The Gabriel can be mounted either in fixed single or trainable triple-cell launchers. Before firing, the missiles guidance system is programmed with target data obtained from the launch platform's own sensors.

A Gabriel Mk II is launched. Prior to the introduction of the longer-range Mk II, Israeli missile craft had to close to within the optimum firing range of the 'Styx'-equipped Arab missile boats, using ECM and AA fire to defend themselves.

and hangar. Though the latter is removable for the alternative fit of more armament, somewhat surprisingly it does not appear to be telescopic. Despite the increase in length, the 'Alia' craft are still very small and their motion must severely limit their freedom to launch and, more importantly, to recover their helicopter.

As with most navies that design and build, that of Israel is tending to produce successively larger classes. The 'Alia' craft are near the upper limit of what can be termed FACs, and a class of 253-ft (77-m) corvettes is believed to be planned. These, at 1,000 tons, would be displacement vessels with cruising diesels and a gas turbine for sprint speeds. Though these would offer a steadier weapon and helicopter platform, together with space for improved command and control facilities, the great increase in dimensions has to be an unwelcome step.

Israeli naval operations call more often for speed rather than endurance and the hydrofoil is, therefore,

attractive. A recent acquisition has been the 83.6-ft (25.5-m) Grumman-built *Shimrit*, whose four-Harpoon/two-Gabriel fit is very respectable for her size, but whose main value lies in the combination of her large, home-built surveillance radar and a 50-kt speed. These will enable her to operate independent of the main force in a reconnaissance early-warning and, possibly, mid-course guidance capacity. Her sole defence lies in her speed and the pair of BMARC 30-mm cannon that have lately been adopted in place of the venerable 40-mm Bofors. A second craft is being built in Israel and more may follow.

Strong opposition

With the likely opposition becoming more sophisticated (Libya with the 125-mile/200-km Otomat SSM and Syria reportedly acquiring Soviet-built 'Nanuckha' vessels with the 31-mile/50-km SS-N-2B), there is more emphasis of late on defensive measures. Beside those implicit in surveillance radar and helicopters, chaff

'Reshef' (or 'Saar 4') class fast missile craft

The 'Reshef' (or 'Saar 4') class of steel hulled missile boat was produced after the Saar 1/2 sub-groups in order to perform the longer range missions in the Mediterranean and Red Sea. The first two units, *Reshef* and *Keshet*, were involved in the 1973 Yom Kippur War and were built with air-conditioned quarters, a combat information centre and various Israeli- and Italian-built electronics systems. A total of 10 were built for Israel with two subsequently being sold to Chile, a third new-build unit having just been ordered for that country. South Africa had three built in Israel and undertook the licence-building of a further six.

Specification
Displacement: 450 tons full load
Dimensions: length 190.6 ft (58.1 m); beam 24.9 ft (7.6 m); draught 8 ft (2.4 m)
Propulsion: four diesels delivering 14,000 hp (10440 kW) to four shafts

Speed: 32 kts
Complement: 45
Armament: one Barak point defence SAM system, four single Gabriel Mk II SSM launchers, two quadruple Harpoon SSM launchers, one or two 76-mm (3-in) dual-purpose guns, none or one single 40-mm AA gun; two single 20-mm AA, three twin 12.7-mm (0.5-in) machine-guns
Electronics: one Thomson-CSF Neptune TH-D1040 radar, one Selenia Orion RTN-10X radar, one Elta MN-53 ECM system, four chaff/decoy rocket launchers and (in some) one ELAC sonar

To increase the ASW capabilities of her navy Israel has equipped a number of her 'Dabur' class coastal patrol craft with two single 324-mm Mk 32 torpedo tubes for the American 45-kt, 6.8-mile (11-km) range Mk 46 torpedo.

Israel Shipyards Corvette

In order to markedly improve the command and control of the missile boat squadrons and the coastal ASW defences Israel is believed to be building a small number of general purpose and ASW corvettes to a 'Saar 5' design prepared by Israel Shipyards, Haifa. Both versions will be able to carry a light helicopter for over-the-horizon missile targeting, SSM decoy operations and ASW missions, a role that was first tried out on a 'Reshef' class missile boat and incorporated into several of the 'Alia' class vessels.

Specification (provisional)
'Saar 5' class
Displacement: 1,000 tons full load
Dimensions: length 253.2 ft (77.2 m);

beam 28.9 ft (8.8 m); draught 13.8 ft (4.2 m)
Propulsion: combined diesel and gas turbine driving two shafts
Speed: 42 kts
Complement: 45
Aircraft: one light helicopter
Armament: (GP version) one Barak point defence SAM system, two quadruple Harpoon SSM launchers, two single 76-mm (3-in) dual-purpose guns, two twin 30-mm AA guns; (ASW version) four single Gabriel Mk II/III SSM launchers, two single 76-mm (3-in) dual-purpose guns, one triple 375-mm Bofors ASW rocket launcher, two triple 424-mm Mk 32 ASW torpedo tubes (12 Mk 46 torpedoes)
Electronics: not known at present

launchers are being carried in generous numbers, ECM antennae are proliferating and the American Vulcan/Phalanx CIWS is being purchased for installation on the larger and later units. Though full-size anti-surface ship torpedoes can be carried by all the 'Saar' classes, they are rarely seen because of their unsuitability against small, fast targets.

A smaller class of craft, the 65.6-ft (20 m) 'Dabur' type, is also in service, up to 35 being reported. Not particularly fast, they are used for patrol purposes and, interestingly, are the largest that can feasibly be transported overland between the Mediterranean and the Gulf of Aqaba.

The Israeli fleet is primarily an offensive force, unsuited for the purpose of protecting the state's not inconsiderable mercantile traffic. This must be vulnerable to attack by submarines and mines. Despite their token sonars and anti-submarine torpedoes, FACs make poor ASW craft and the corvettes will be more

useful in the role. Following experience with ex-British submarines, Israel acquired three small IKL-designed boats of its own in 1977. Lying somewhere between the Types 205 and 206 of the Bundesmarine, these have a greater buoyancy reserve. Political considerations again demanded construction outside West Germany, and the boats were built in considerable secrecy by Vickers in the UK. Like the Germans' own boats, they are designed for short-endurance work in restricted waters and carry a heavy eight-tube torpedo battery. It is reported that there is interest in the acquisition of three larger boats, possibly derivatives of the Type 209, exported successfully worldwide and operated by near-neighbours Greece and Turkey, of which the latter is also building the type.

About a dozen tank landing craft are operated for small-scale amphibious operations. These would need to be conducted under conditions of total air superiority, for supporting craft currently have nothing

Below: Included in the navy's order of battle is a Commando of 300 men who are highly trained for covert raiding operations using parachutes, small craft, frogmen suits or swimmer delivery vehicles.

Left: Thirty-five 'Dabur' class coastal patrol craft are used by the Israeli navy. In recent years they have seen extensive use against Palestinian guerrilla incursions from the sea.

A 'Saar-2' class missile boat with two triple Gabriel launcher cells. This sub-class has since been refitted with a pair of Harpoon SSM launchers in place of one cell, and called the 'Saar-3' class.

larger than 3-in (76-mm) guns for fire support, and all too little defensive firepower to counter a determined aerial attack.

A naval commando is included in the order of battle but would probably be used either in small raiding groups or to seize features vital to the success of a landing.

What the Israelis obviously lack is a credible mine-countermeasures force. Their shallow approaches are admirably suited to a mining campaign and ground-laid influence mines are readily available from Soviet sources. These can be launched from a variety of

vehicles including the small coasters that infest the Levant. Highly cost-effective, mines are simply laid but expensive and disruptively time-consuming to clear; the threat should be taken seriously.

The Israeli navy is in good shape and is more than a match for any Arab fleet in terms of numbers, firepower and training. Because of this, however, it would be reasonable to assume that potential opponents would seek to neutralize it by other means and, currently, Israel's navy would not appear to be too well equipped to deal with a well co-ordinated aerial attack employing the new generation of missiles.

Type 206 Coastal Submarine

Built for political reasons in great secrecy by Vickers in the UK, the three Type 206 coastal submarines *Gal, Rahav* and *Tanin* are in fact a West German IKL design. They carry a main battery of eight 21-in (533-mm) bow torpedo tubes for 19-in (483-mm) NT37C 34-kt (20-km) range dual anti-ship/ASW torpedoes, and are fitted for, but do not carry, the Vickers Blowpipe SLAM anti-aircraft missile system for submarines. The class is used as hunter-killers against Arab sub-surface craft and are tasked with providing covert delivery of Naval Commando units to Arab coastal targets. Israel is known to be interested in procuring a similar number of larger submarines for longer range operations.

Specification
Displacement: 420 tons surface, 600 tons dived
Dimensions: 146.7 ft (45 m); beam 15.4 ft (4.7 m); draught 12 ft (3.7 m)
Propulsion: diesel-electric drive with one shaft
Speed: 11 kts surface, 17 kts dived
Complement: 22
Armament: eight 21-in (533-mm) bow torpedo tubes (10 NT37C torpedoes), fitted for, but not with, Blowpipe-SLAM anti-aircraft SAM system.
Electronics: not known

INDEX

Page numbers indicating a picture are in **bold**

Picture Acknowledgements

The publishers are grateful to the following people and organisations for their help in supplying photographs for this book.

Orbis Publishing Ltd: Pages 4, 5, 6 (x 2), 7 (x 2), 8 (x 2), 9 (x 3), 12
Associated Press: Pages 10, 14, 15, 16, 17, 18, 19, 20, 21, 22 (x 2), 23, 29, 30, 34 (x 2), 35 (x 2), 51, 52, 53, 54, 61, 63, 66, 67, 104
N.D.: Pages 11, 13, 18, 19, 24, 27, 28 (x 2), 38 (x 2), 41, 50
Fleet Air Arm Museum: Page 23
Keystone Press Agency: Pages 25, 31, 39, 40, 49, 51
Gamma: Pages 26, 29, 37, 41, 45 (x 2), 49, 56, 60, 66, 67, 68, 72, 73, 77, 79, 83, 86, 87, 88, 99, 108, 120, 121, 157
R.F.: Pages 30, 36, 39, 40 (x 2), 52, 58, 69, 70 (x 2), 71, 72, 73, 78, 81, 82 (x 2), 83, 85, 88, 89 (x 2), 92, 93, 94, 95, 96, 98, 100 (x 2), 102, 104, 105
Israel Defence Forces: Pages 58, 61, 80, 95, 115, 116, 126 (x 2), 130, 141, 148, 150, 153, 156
Israel Aircraft Industries: Pages 59, 62, 107, 111 (x 2), 115, 128, 149, 151, 152, 153
Eshel Dramit: Pages 76, 105, 125, 144
Israel Military Industries: Pages 98, 101 (x 2), 102, 103, 104
McDonnell Douglas Corporation: Pages 106, 127
Denys Hughes: Pages 110, 125, 129, 132, 133, 136, 137, 142, 143 (x 2), 145 (x 2), 146, 147
Ligad Rotloy
Meir Meiselman
Mike Mireham
Herzel Konsari
Gil Arbel (Israeli air force)